# ARBITRARY BORDERS

## Political Boundaries in World History

**The Division of the Middle East**
The Treaty of Sèvres

**The Iron Curtain**
The Cold War in Europe

**The Mason–Dixon Line**

**Vietnam: The 17th Parallel**

**Korea: The 38th Parallel**

**The U.S.–Mexico Border**
The Treaty of Guadalupe Hidalgo

D0075416

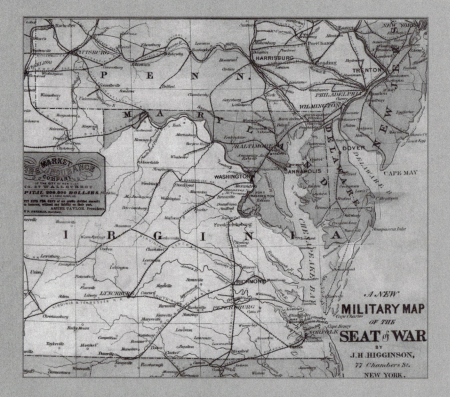

**ARBITRARY BORDERS**

Political Boundaries in World History

# The Mason-Dixon Line

John C. Davenport

**Foreword by**
Senator **George J. Mitchell**

**Introduction by**
**James I. Matray**
California State University, Chico

**CHELSEA HOUSE**
P U B L I S H E R S
A Haights Cross Communications Company

Philadelphia

FRONTIS   The dotted line between Pennsylvania and Maryland shows the location of the Mason-Dixon Line.

## CHELSEA HOUSE PUBLISHERS

VP, NEW PRODUCT DEVELOPMENT   Sally Cheney
DIRECTOR OF PRODUCTION   Kim Shinners
CREATIVE MANAGER   Takeshi Takahashi
MANUFACTURING MANAGER   Diann Grasse

### Staff for THE MASON-DIXON LINE

EXECUTIVE EDITOR   Lee Marcott
PRODUCTION EDITOR   Megan Emery
ASSISTANT PHOTO EDITOR   Noelle Nardone
INTERIOR DESIGN   Keith Trego
COVER DESIGNER   Keith Trego
LAYOUT   EJB Publishing Services

A Haights Cross Communications Company

Librarywww.chelseahouse.com

First Printing

9 8 7 6 5 4 3 2 1

Library of Congress Cataloging-in-Publication Data
applied for.

ISBN: 0-7910-7830-2

# Contents

# Foreword

Senator **George J. Mitchell**

I spent years working for peace in Northern Ireland and in the Middle East. I also made many visits to the Balkans during the long and violent conflict there.

Each of the three areas is unique; so is each conflict. But there are also some similarities: in each, there are differences over religion, national identity, and territory.

Deep religious differences that lead to murderous hostility are common in human history. Competing aspirations involving national identity are more recent occurrences, but often have been just as deadly.

Territorial disputes—two or more people claiming the same land—are as old as humankind. Almost without exception, such disputes have been a factor in recent conflicts. It is impossible to calculate the extent to which the demand for land—as opposed to religion, national identity, or other factors— figures in the motivation of people caught up in conflict. In my experience it is a substantial factor that has played a role in each of the three conflicts mentioned above.

In Northern Ireland and the Middle East, the location of the border was a major factor in igniting and sustaining the conflict. And it is memorialized in a dramatic and visible way: through the construction of large walls whose purpose is to physically separate the two communities.

In Belfast, the capital and largest city in Northern Ireland, the so-called "Peace Line" cuts through the heart of the city, right across urban streets. Up to thirty feet high in places, topped with barbed wire in others, it is an ugly reminder of the duration and intensity of the conflict.

In the Middle East, as I write these words, the government of Israel has embarked on a huge and controversial effort to construct a security fence roughly along the line that separates Israel from the West Bank.

Having served a tour of duty with the U.S. Army in Berlin, which was once the site of the best known of modern walls, I am skeptical of their long-term value, although they often serve short-term needs. But it cannot be said that such structures represent a new idea. Ancient China built the Great Wall to deter nomadic Mongol tribes from attacking its population.

In much the same way, other early societies established boundaries and fortified them militarily to achieve the goal of self-protection. Borders always have separated people. Indeed, that is their purpose.

This series of books examines the important and timely issue of the significance of arbitrary borders in history. Each volume focuses attention on a territorial division, but the analytical approach is more comprehensive. These studies describe arbitrary borders as places where people interact differently from the way they would if the boundary did not exist. This pattern is especially pronounced where there is no geographic reason for the boundary and no history recognizing its legitimacy. Even though many borders have been defined without legal precision, governments frequently have provided vigorous monitoring and military defense for them.

This series will show how the migration of people and exchange of goods almost always work to undermine the separation that borders seek to maintain. The continuing evolution of a European community provides a contemporary example illustrating this point, most obviously with the adoption of a single currency. Moreover, even former Soviet bloc nations have eliminated barriers to economic and political integration.

Globalization has emerged as one of the most powerful forces in international affairs during the twenty-first century. Not only have markets for the exchange of goods and services become genuinely worldwide, but instant communication and sharing of information have shattered old barriers separating people. Some scholars even argue that globalization has made the entire concept of a territorial nation-state irrelevant. Although the assertion is certainly premature and probably wrong, it highlights the importance of recognizing how borders often have reflected and affirmed the cultural, ethnic, or linguistic perimeters that define a people or a country.

Since the Cold War ended, competition over resources or a variety of interests threaten boundaries more than ever, resulting in contentious interaction, conflict, adaptation, and intermixture. How people define their borders is also a factor in determining how events develop in the surrounding region. This series will provide detailed descriptions of selected arbitrary borders in history with the objective of providing insights on how artificial boundaries separating people will influence international affairs during the next century.

Senator George J. Mitchell
October 2003

# Introduction

James I. Matray
California State University, Chico

Throughout history, borders have separated people. Scholars have devoted considerable attention to assessing the significance and impact of territorial boundaries on the course of human history, explaining how they often have been sources of controversy and conflict. In the modern age, the rise of nation-states in Europe created the need for governments to negotiate treaties to confirm boundary lines that periodically changed as a consequence of wars and revolutions. European expansion in the nineteenth century imposed new borders on Africa and Asia. Many native peoples viewed these boundaries as arbitrary and, after independence, continued to contest their legitimacy. At the end of both world wars in the twentieth century, world leaders drew artificial and impermanent lines separating assorted people around the globe. Borders certainly are among the most important factors that have influenced the development of world affairs.

Chelsea House Publishers decided to publish a collection of books looking at arbitrary borders in history in response to the revival of the nuclear crisis in North Korea in October 2002. Recent tensions on the Korean peninsula are a direct consequence of the partitioning of Korea at the 38th parallel after World War II. Other nations in the course of human history have suffered due to similar artificial divisions. The reasons for establishing arbitrary borders have differed, but usually arise from either domestic or international factors and are often a combination of both. In the case of Korea, it was the United States and the Soviet Union who decided in August 1945 to partition the country at the 38th parallel. Ostensibly, the purpose was to facilitate the acceptance of the surrender of Japanese forces at the end of World War II. However, historians have presented persuasive evidence that a political contest existed inside Korea to decide the future of the nation after forty years of Japanese colonial rule. Therefore, Korea's division at the 38th parallel was an artificial boundary that symbolized the split among the Korean people about the nation's destiny. On the right were conservative landowners who had closely aligned with the Japanese, many of whom were outright collaborators. On the left, there were far more individuals who favored revolutionary change. In fact, Communists provided the leadership and direction for the independence movement inside Korea from the 1920s until the end of World War II. After 1945, two Koreas emerged that reflected these divergent ideologies. But the Korean people have never accepted the legitimacy or permanence of the division imposed by foreign powers.

Korea's experience in dealing with the artificial division of its country may well be unique, but it is not without historical parallels. The first set of books in this series on arbitrary borders examines six key chapters in human history. One volume will look at the history of the 38th parallel in Korea. Other volumes will provide description and analysis of the division of the Middle East after World War I; the Cold War as symbolized by the Iron Curtain in Central Europe; the United States.-Mexico Border; the 17th parallel in Vietnam, and the Mason-Dixon Line. Future books will address the Great Wall in China, Northern Ireland's border, and the Green Line in Israel. Admittedly, there are many significant differences between these boundaries, but these books will cover as many common themes as possible. In so doing, each will help readers conceptualize how factors such as colonialism, culture, and economics determine the nature of contact between people along these borders. Although globalization has emerged as a powerful force working against the creation and maintenance of lines separating people, boundaries are not likely to disappear as factors with a continuing influence on world events. This series of books will provide insights about the impact of arbitrary borders on human history and how such borders continue to shape the modern world.

James I. Matray
Chico, California
November 2003

# 1

# Gettysburg
# November, 1863

As he stood in front of the assembled audience, Abraham Lincoln could feel the sadness and sacredness of the place. He had planned only a short address for that brisk fall morning, a mere 272 words in all, or about three minutes' worth of speaking time, "a few appropriate remarks," as Lincoln's invitation indicated, to dedicate a cemetery.[1] The president did not deceive himself into believing that anything he could say would relieve the pain of his listeners or somehow magically transform this occasion into a celebration. This was no place for celebration, perhaps not even commemoration. Terrible things had happened on this field, acts of violence that stripped away civilization, revealed the worst side of what it meant to be human, and broke the heart of a compassionate man like Lincoln. Then again, the president and the country had already endured over two and a half years of suffering and pain as the nation tore itself apart in civil war. Tragedy was nothing new. One man could say precious little to wipe away the tears of millions.

On battlefields great and small, the flower of an entire generation had fallen. From Shiloh in the West to Charleston along the Atlantic Coast, men had fought and died. White and black, Northerner and Southerner, their blood flowed too easily for convictions concerning the future direction of the nation.. This war they were caught up in was to decide the orientation of the country's moral compass. In which direction would the compass needle point—North or South? Only blood, it turned out, could settle the matter. Americans surely had grown accustomed to terrible things. The cemetery at Gettysburg, Pennsylvania, was only one of too many resting places for America's war dead, men who had sacrificed their lives in the service of ideas on which they based their identities, but about which they understood precious little. Yes, Lincoln's address would be brief; a grieving nation did not need more.

Lincoln's audience did indeed grieve, and they remembered. They knew well what had transpired that previous summer on the green fields on which they stood and in the lush, copper-hued woods that enveloped them on this serene autumn day. A

President Lincoln stands here with several Union generals at the headquarters of the Army of the Potomac in this photograph taken during the Civil War. The Union victory was bittersweet for Lincoln who lamented the enduring pain, destruction, and separation the war inflicted on the country.

few short months before, soldiers had milled about, preparing to give their all on this very ground. Some proud and defiant, others angry, most simply frightened, the men came to fight. Equipped with the most modern weapons available and secure in the morality of their conflicting causes, soldiers and officers on both sides confronted the terror of the moment. Trying to hide their fear, men anxiously awaited their leaders' hoarse cries of "Forward, boys!" Dreading battle and blind to the day, the soldiers most likely never considered the contrasting colors of the battlefield—the greens and browns of the earth, the woody tints of the patches of forest, the softly shading blue of the sky. They might have even ignored the different colors of the uniforms they wore. Yet here, too, one could not miss the contrasts.

On one side of the soon-to-be bloody field, long lines of forlorn figures marched back and forth, forming and re-forming their ranks in anticipation of the fight. Many of these men wore outfits of dull, dirty gray; others were clad in butternut brown. Still others were dressed in the same clothes they enlisted in, with only a gray cap to mark their allegiance. No matter the arrangement, the colors meant something, identified the men as being from a particular place and embracing a shared set of social, cultural, and political assumptions. The men would defend those assumptions and their place of origin with assorted weapons of war—.58-caliber rifled muskets firing lethally accurate bullets; cannons leveled at the enemy, launching grapeshot and canister rounds like huge shotguns; howitzers capable of arching exploding shells behind their opponents' lines. Among the mass of fighting men and equipment, officers paraded about on prancing horses from the finest breeding farms of Kentucky and Virginia, looking resplendent and dashing in their dark gray coats, yellow sashlike belts, and glistening black knee-high boots. The flags that fluttered behind them as they barked orders to subordinates and set about the task at hand carried the stars and bars of a rebel government. The officers commanded a collection of soldiers drawn from all over the American South, including Virginia, Alabama, Georgia, and South Carolina.

The men of this army came from small farms, large plantations, cities, and towns to defend a way of life unique to their part of the country, a culture and society built on the foundation of human slavery. They sought the perpetuation of a belief system peculiar to their homeland, peculiar to a South that existed in their dreams and hopes. This was the Army of Northern Virginia, commanded by General Robert E. Lee. The men on this side of the field at Gettysburg carried with them a shared sense of a uniquely Southern nationality. As one sergeant from Georgia told his wife on the eve of battle, should he fall she must not mourn him, "knowing that if I am killed that I die fighting for my country and my rights."[2] Gettysburg became this man's grave, as it did for so many other young Southerners who had prepared themselves to fight and die for a geographical figment of the imagination called the Confederate States of America.

Opposite Lee's army stood men and boys equally frightened of what lay ahead that day. Like deadly dance partners, these blue-clad troops shifted their lines again and again to remain in step with their adversaries. Here and there, officers in bright blue coats, girdled with thick leather belts from which hung long sabers and .44-caliber pistols, galloped around the field, moving the ever-flowing ribbon of blue into line. As the soldiers jostled into position, their rifled muskets, crowned by gleaming, nearly two-foot-long bayonets, rose up like needles. Artillery pieces, drawn by teams of horses and tended by men equipped with an array of swabs, rams, screws, and buckets of water, clattered behind the ranks, ready to shower the Confederate troops with their deadly load. The majesty of the moment overwhelmed a young cannoneer, who thrilled in "watching these splendid soldiers ... their muskets glittering in the rays of the sun."[3]

Slowly, order emerged as soldiers from Minnesota, Ohio, Indiana, and just about every other state in the North watched regimental standards unfurl to the accompaniment of blaring bugles and beating drums. No sooner had the covers been removed than the standards began to wave in the summer breeze. Impressive and inspiring though they were, none surpassed in majesty the brilliant flags of red, white, and blue that reminded the soldiers of their cause. No banner that day could match the star-spangled one that symbolized yet another geographical fiction, the United States of America. This banner represented of ideas and beliefs utterly antagonistic to those of Lee's men. The flag stood for cultural and social assumptions that had evolved to their fullest extent in what was known as the North, a place set in clear opposition to its counterpart known as the South. The North possessed an illusory topography that had shape only in the minds of the men who put on the blue uniform of the federal government. This was the Army of the Potomac, under the command of General George Meade, and it stood ready to defend the Constitution against its greatest challenge. Meade brought his men to Gettysburg prepared to make the ultimate sacrifice to preserve the Union and guarantee freedom for all Americans regardless of the color of their skin.

Men from the North had come to this spot to fight men from the South in a contest over principles, values, and institutions that had evolved along separate paths for almost 200 years. Through the first half of this country's history as an independent nation, two separate Americas had been establishing themselves. The worldviews on which each America had been founded were unique and almost incomprehensible to fellow citizens living in the geographic "other." This fact was both amplified by and dependent on an imagined border between the two halves of what was technically one country. This border did not so much separate political entities as it did people and mindsets. Two distinct ways of seeing the world, and constructing societies to fit, existed on opposite sides of a dividing line that began near the shores of the Chesapeake Bay and, in one form or another, continued to California.

The armies of the Confederacy and the Union were determined to protect distinct cultural identities that had been constructed along regional, geographically defined lines over time and that had developed in divergent directions to the point where differences became irreconcilable. This fundamental clash led to war. The soldiers commanded by Lee and Meade, in other words, chose sides and were willing to give up their lives for ideas and beliefs associated with two places that existed on opposite sides of a single imaginary line, a line that ran through hearts and minds. This border that drove one people, with common roots and a shared history, into warring camps had transcended maps and transformed brothers into implacable foes. It was a line of humble origins meant to settle a relatively minor dispute about which the soldiers assembled in Pennsylvania that July knew little and cared less. No one could have imagined the destructive power and historical impact of one simple line on a piece of paper. The cold stone markers that made that line into

a border between two American colonies and later two states—
when viewed almot 100 years after their placement—resembled
eerily the gravestones that would soon testify to the carnage of
the battle of Gettysburg. The firing lines that the Confederate
and Union troops pulled themselves into became the deadliest
chapter in the history of a line drawn by a pair of obscure
English astronomers named Mason and Dixon.

# 2

# Two Plans,
# One Place

England got into the colonial game a bit later than its European rivals. The Spanish and French had already begun exploiting the riches of the New World by the time England planted its first outpost in Virginia in 1607. Slow off the mark though they were, the English soon caught up to and eventually surpassed their Continental neighbors. Staking claims in North America proved to be the easy part, though; laying out their contours and boundaries was quite another matter. Colonies needed charters, and charters needed to specify the exact borders of the proposed settlements to avoid land disputes arising out of overlapping administrative authority. Ideally, the borders between colonies would be set accurately in London prior to the actual settlement of the areas in question, but England was 3,000 miles away from America. As a result, colonial boundaries were often either hopelessly vague or haphazardly drawn. Charter holders thus found themselves in constant conflict and occasionally even in litigation over where each other's land began and ended.

One of the earliest charters granted by the English crown went to Massachusetts. Written in 1629, one year before the great Puritan migration, the charter gave the new inhabitants an ill-defined region that encompassed "all those Landes ... North and South [of the Charles River] in Latitude and Breadth, and in Length and Longitude ... the mayne Landes there, from the Atlantick and Western Sea and Ocean ... to the South Sea."[4] The settlers were understandably unsure of where their new home was located. The reference to longitude would have been even more baffling given the fact that no one had yet discovered how to measure it accurately. Latitude was easy enough to determine. One could use any number of sextants or astrolabes to find out where one stood in relation to the poles, how one stood north or south of the equator. Saying with any certainty one's location east or west, however, was a far different proposition. In the seventeenth and eighteenth centuries, in fact, it was rather a matter of guesswork. At least the Puritans knew where to start. Virginia's charter of 1606 simply told the colonists to settle "at any Place upon said Coast of *Virginia* or *America,* where they

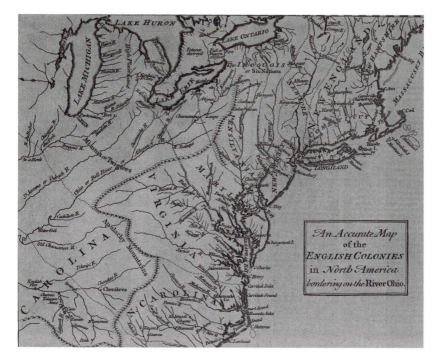

Though England was late in entering the colonial game, its North American presence soon became widespread. This 1754 map shows the English colonies extending from Maine to South Carolina in the south and Lake Michigan in the west.

should think fit and convenient."[5] Such imprecise instructions were repeated time and again, and doomed the settlers to ceaseless border disputes.

Of course, the lines that royal authorities seemed so inept at laying out were often drawn by other hands. Nature's pen sometimes proved to be more reliable. Throughout North America, but perhaps most sharply in the region along the Mid-Atlantic Coast known as the Chesapeake or, a bit farther to the south, the Tidewater, geography limited the area available for settlement and cultivation, and established unofficial borders that the English were initially compelled to recognize. To the east of the great bay that gave the place its name lay the ocean the colonists had just sailed across, an ocean crucial to their survival. The sea meant trade, and trade ensured lasting success for any colonial venture. All the English colonies possessed a commercial component; they were expected at some point to pay for themselves by supplying the parent country with valuable raw resources and by consuming finished goods. Access to the ocean trade routes necessitated a coastal orientation. The colonies were tethered to the shores of the Atlantic whether they chose to be or not.

Trade, in turn, depended on the exploitation of inland forests and farmland. These parts could be accessed most profitably via the region's rivers, which served as a vast network of highways. Plantations far from the coastal harbors, often situated along the rivers' banks to take advantage of the rich alluvial soil, could export crops and other produce and import finished goods using relatively inexpensive, reliable river transport. These waterways, however, were navigable only up to the fall line, where the land began to rise up into the Appalachian Mountains, the rocky spine of eastern North America. With highlands to the west, the open sea to the east, and commercially viable farmland confined primarily to the rivers' margins, the colonists' options were rather limited. This state of affairs exaggerated the significance of determining boundaries and surveying lines. Arable land capable of turning a profit could never be taken for granted; precious little of it was available. Establishing just who possessed what, and where, remained central to any American enterprise.

Further limitations were imposed by the land's native residents. Although coastal Indians had been either evicted or subjugated by the mid–seventeenth century, their inland counterparts remained unyielding. Much like the potent Iroquois Confederacy in the north, the Susquehanna and Delaware tribes of the Mid-Atlantic region clung tenaciously to their ancestral homes and restrained any English impulse to settle beyond the Appalachian barrier. They, too, were farmers and valued their fields as much as any English farmer. Land purchases, of course, could be negotiated on a local basis, but the line between European and Native American holdings remained frustratingly impenetrable. Too often, for English tastes, settlers were relegated to Indian leftovers when it came to land. As one

Virginia farmer said in the 1630s, the English generally gained "possession of no more ground than [Indian] waste."[6] Parceling out equitably what little was available thus became paramount. Competition for scarce space made clear boundaries and borders essential to the colonial project.

The need for lines of demarcation in colonial America grew in urgency as the colonists grew in numbers. Between 1625 and 1630, the population of Virginia, still concentrated in the Tidewater area, nearly doubled,[7] increasing the pressure on the land and straining relations between the colonists. News that another batch of immigrants soon would arrive and head for the coastal area farther up the Chesapeake Bay did not sit well with the Virginians. More settlers meant more competition for available land. Yet arrive they did, novice planters to work the soil in the hope of profiting from America's bounty. Wealth, however, was not this group's primary motivation. Unlike their counterparts in Virginia, these additions to the colonial mix were religious dissenters, Roman Catholics seeking a refuge where they could worship, and prosper, in safety.

Catholics made up a suspect minority back home in seventeenth-century England. The Anglican majority feared and distrusted them, and routinely discriminated against men and women they called "papists." Still, Catholic fortunes waxed and waned with the shifts in English politics. During the second half of the sixteenth century, Catholics gained favor and temporary ascendancy during the reign of Queen Mary I. Under her sister, Elizabeth I, however, Anglican leaders hounded and persecuted English Catholics. The Stuart monarchy, which began with James I in 1603, witnessed a return to tolerance and the opening of limited opportunities to the Catholic minority. James I and his son, Charles I, took a soft position on Catholicism because Catholics represented far less of a threat to Anglican High Church power than did dissenting Protestants such as the Puritans. The Catholic nobility, in particular, acquired a new degree of influence at the royal court. George Calvert, Lord Baltimore, counted himself among this number. Calvert was fascinated by America and viewed settlement there in terms of both profit and sanctuary. He envisioned a Catholic colony in the New World that would prosper within the English economic framework while simultaneously offering a haven to his persecuted fellow Catholics. Calvert's slice of America would make money and rescue a harassed people from the changing fortunes of life in England.

Beginning in 1630, Calvert tried to use his influence at the court of Charles I to gain a personal land grant, known as a proprietorship, just north of the Virginia colony. After years of lobbying, Calvert's petition finally succeeded in June 1632. The first Lord Baltimore, unfortunately, could not savor his victory; he had died the preceding April, leaving his son, Cecilius, in possession of the proprietary grant. Cecilius, second Lord Baltimore, gratefully named his new holding after Charles I's queen consort, Henrietta Maria. The colony would be called Maryland. Two years later, 300 optimistic and energetic settlers arrived on the shores of the Chesapeake. America had a new batch of English planters—and a new set of boundaries to squabble over.

Calvert's people quickly took up the task of defining the colony's borders and the settlers' new American identity. One of their first actions was to declare a policy of religious toleration; it was, after all, the driving force behind the entire project, but economic matters occupied the Marylanders' attention as well. Baltimore instructed his people to treat Virginia's Protestants, and any Protestants already among the Maryland immigrants, "with as much mildness and favor as Justice will permit." The settlers were to make their homes not only where it was "probable to be healthful and fruitful," but also at a place they deemed "convenient for trade." Calvert reminded the colonists that one of their tasks was to research the possibility of mining various ores and "find out what other commodities may probably be made."[8] No matter how just or holy, a colony had to survive in the real world. Its inhabitants needed to develop and grow a sound and efficient economic base.

Maryland's borders were as ill defined as any in America; settlements up and down the Atlantic Coast struggled to establish clear boundaries. One thing, however, was for sure: Maryland was indisputably Southern. From a very early date, the colony positioned itself to take advantage of the Tidewater's primary cash crop, tobacco. Much like its neighbor to the south, Virginia, Maryland welcomed an export economy dependent for the main part on a single product. As they were established, other Southern colonies would do likewise. In the late seventeenth century, the Carolinas would add rice and indigo to the list of Southern cash crops; Georgia would contribute much of the same. Mirroring the process already underway in Virginia, Maryland pursued an economy based on tobacco. In 1697, the Maryland assembly succinctly stated the reality of the colony's economy: "The trade of this province ebbs and flows according to the rise or fall in the market of England."[9] Indeed, tobacco sustained both Virginia and Maryland until the American Revolution. The average farmer in the Chesapeake drew anywhere from 10 to 25 percent of his income from tobacco alone.[10]

Tobacco, like any other cash crop, required intensive cultivation and care. Relying on it as the foundation for a regional economy demanded a substantial work force that the Chesapeake did not have. Almost from its founding, Maryland suffered from an acute labor shortage. The situation worsened as time passed. For most of the seventeenth century, Maryland and Virginia tried to remedy matters by employing white workers bound to individual planters through a system of contract labor known as indentured servitude. Indentured servitude, however, was a cumbersome institution that promised only a relatively short-term solution to the colony's growing need for strong hands to work the soil. A far more economical labor system presented itself in the form of African slavery. As Maryland matured, its plantations and farms came to depend increasingly on black slaves as the primary work force. This dependency aligned Maryland ever more closely with Virginia and the other Southern colonist, and initiated the process of forging a distinctly Southern identity and outlook within the colony's as yet vaguely drawn borders.

The story of William Penn's colonial venture follows a somewhat similar path but with a very different developmental

## FOR GOD AND PROFIT

Like Pennsylvania and Maryland, several other English colonies began as mixed ventures designed to make money while providing refuge for religious minorities. Massachusetts, Connecticut, and Rhode Island were all established with both profit and God in mind. Massachusetts was the first in 1629. There the Puritan leader John Winthrop hoped to create a godly and prosperous community of the faithful that would act as a "city upon a hill,"* as Winthrop said it, radiating God's grace while turning a handsome profit for the colony's mercantile elite. Among Massachusetts's most aggressive entrepreneurs were Winthrop's son and grandsons, who came to dominate the land market in southern New England. Connecticut split off from Massachusetts in 1635, partly due to population pressures but also because of discord within older congregations in Massachusetts. Once established along the banks of the Connecticut River, the transplanted English settlers worshipped in a manner of their own choosing and developed a lucrative fur trade with the local Indians. An attempt to monopolize this trade generated tensions that led to a bloody war that resulted in the near extermination of the Pequot Indians. Religious dissidents who rejected the authority of the established Puritan hierarchy founded Rhode Island in 1636. Driven out of Boston and led by the minister Roger Williams, Rhode Island's settlers focused on self-government, religious tolerance, and living in peace with their Native American neighbors during the early decades of the colony's existence, but they soon turned to fishing, shipping, and eventually the slave trade as engines to drive the local economy. The colony retained its reputation for free thinking and tolerance but enmeshed itself deeply in the Atlantic trade. Religion, economics, and politics often intersected and blended in colonial America. As John Frederick Martin has written, in New England, as well as Pennsylvania and Maryland, the "pious and the commercial existed alongside each other...."**

*Jack P. Greene, ed., *Settlements to Society: A Documentary History of Colonial America* (New York: W.W. Norton and Company, 1975), 68.

**John Frederick Martin, *Profits in the Wilderness: Entrepreneurship and the Founding of the New England Towns in the Seventeenth Century* (Chapel Hill: University of North Carolina Press, 1991), 302.

end point. Born in 1644, Penn entered life as the son of a well-connected English admiral, Sir William Penn. The senior Penn had been favored by King Charles II, son of the monarch who issued the Maryland grant to Calvert. Admiral Penn gave his support to Charles II during the latter's campaign to restore the English crown to the Stuart line, after a bitter civil war and subsequent commonwealth had removed it between 1649 and 1660. Penn supported Charles personally and politically but demonstrated his loyalty in tangible terms by loaning the Stuart king a sizable sum of money. After his father's death, the younger Penn found himself holding the king's debt and thus in prime position to negotiate a favorable settlement, one that just might allow him to realize a cherished and long-held dream.

Like his soon-to-be neighbor Calvert, Penn belonged to a religious minority that had endured years of discrimination and persecution in England, in this instance the Society of Friends, or the Quakers as they were called. As a youth, Penn had drifted into the simple-living, quietly egalitarian, pacifist sect. He found himself enamored of its message of honest faith and its emphasis on community. By 1680, he was in a position to bestow upon his fellow Quakers a gift of inestimable value. Using his considerable influence at the royal court, Penn asked for and received in 1681 an American land grant in exchange for canceling the debt owed to his father by Charles II. The grant gave Penn control over an extensive, though poorly defined, tract of land adjacent to Calvert's Maryland. Located immediately to the north of Lord Baltimore's colony, Penn's holding, in its natural beauty, would reflect the prestige of its proprietor; it was christened Pennsylvania, literally "Penn's woodlands."

Like Calvert, Penn conceived of his colony as both a commercial and a religious enterprise. He envisioned a harmonious community where hardworking small farmers, craftsmen, and their families enjoyed "the rights and freedoms of England [in] a free, just, and industrious colony." By industrious, Penn meant a colony possessing a mixed economy of trade and agriculture where "husband-men and day labourers" mingled freely with merchants. Employing Quaker values as moral and social anchors, Penn saw that commerce and farming could cooperate to produce "good discipline and just government" for "a plain and well intending people."[11] As one Pennsylvania colonist wrote,

> Our business ... here, in this new land is not so much to build houses, and establish factories, and promote trade, that may enrich ourselves (though these things in their due place are not to be neglected) as to erect temples of holiness and right- eousness, which God may delight in; to lay such lasting frames and foundations of temperance and virtue, as may support the superstructures of our future happiness, both in this world, and the other world.[12]

Pennsylvania, like its neighbor Maryland, would root itself firmly in trade and commerce; export markets would have to be identified and exploited. Penn, however, aligned his colony's economy with no single cash crop, no predominant export good. As with colonies such as Massachusetts, Connecticut, Rhode Island, New York, and New Jersey, there would be no one axis around which Pennsylvania's entire economy would spin. In this sense, Pennsylvania's orientation would bear a Northern stamp.

With this firmly fixed vision, Penn arrived to begin his American experiment in October 1682. Immediately, he set about resolving at least one pressing issue involving boundaries. Penn made contact with local Indians and expressed in plain terms his intention to live next to them as a good neighbor. The proprietor impressed on the native inhabitants his desire to coexist peacefully, and he conveyed his sincere respect for them and their culture. Penn exclaimed that the "king of the Country where I live, hath given unto me a Province therein, but I desire to enjoy it with your Love and Consent, that we may always live together as Neighbors and friends...."[13] The line between these two groups would remain sacred as far as Penn was concerned, to be crossed only in amicable commerce.

In 1680, William Penn founded Pennsylvania as a commercial and religious community where colonists could enjoy freedom from religious persecution and strict class structures. Penn immediately contacted local Indians and expressed his respect for their culture and land and his desire to coexist peacefully with them, which eliminated the boundary issues that plagued some other colonies. This 1772 Benjamin West painting shows Penn and other statesmen meeting with the Indians shortly after Pennsylvania's establishment.

Arriving at a similar arrangement with his English neighbor to the south would prove a bit more complicated. If Penn hoped to establish a clear border between the two colonies, he would have to engage in a series of delicate negotiations with Calvert. Two months after his arrival, Penn took the first step in this direction by requesting a meeting with Lord Baltimore to determine a precise line of demarcation between, even at this early date, recognizably different colonial enterprises: the industrious beehive of yeoman farmers, small tradesmen, and ambitious merchants proposed by Penn, on the one hand, and Calvert's tobacco-centered, rigidly hierarchical, plantation economy, very shortly to become dependent on black slave labor, on the other. The proprietors needed to draw a line between emerging realities and identities, a boundary that would recognize yet also amplify alternative patterns of society and culture.

**3**

# One Place, Two Peoples

The dreary winter weather dampened expectations as much as spirits on the December day in 1682 that witnessed the first meeting between Penn and Calvert. The two proprietors chose the town of Annapolis in Maryland as the venue partly because no similarly well appointed meeting place yet existed in Pennsylvania and partly as an expression of deference on Penn's part to his older colonial neighbor. Both Penn and Calvert shared a common goal—to reach agreement on a formal border between their settlements—but each came to the table with different plans on just how to achieve this. Lord Baltimore argued for a line drawn according to a simple measurement along a chosen line of latitude. An easy and common practice, it involved little more than selecting a line close to 40 degrees north, a rough estimate of Maryland's northern boundary, then surveying it westward to the edge of the English pale. Penn, to the contrary, sought a more complex solution. He called for a boundary drawn by a process that required converting latitude into miles between fixed geographic points, and measuring westward from that spot. Neither man felt compelled to compromise, and each chided the other for being hopelessly rigid. The negotiations collapsed, and the meeting adjourned. A follow-up session the next April proved no more fruitful; all it produced was bitterness and frustration.

Finally, both sides agreed to refer the dispute to the authorities in London. There, the Lords Board of Trade, the body responsible for colonial affairs, deliberated and issued a decision, in 1685, that pleased no one. Without explanation, the Lords set the border between Pennsylvania and Maryland exactly at 40 degrees north in a straight line that extended as far west as the Indian lands. England had spoken; it was now up to the Americans to do the work of finding and marking the line on the ground.

Neither Penn nor Calvert moved quickly on the matter because neither accepted the Lords Board of Trade ruling. By the mid–eighteenth century, with both men now dead and the border problem still unresolved, the dispute turned violent. Clashes between farmers in the western parts of both colonies became more frequent and intense because of competition for arable land. Western farmers jealously guarded what little property they had and were willing to assert their claims through violence if necessary. In 1736, for example, 50 Pennsylvania men attacked a Maryland farm, killing the owner in the process. Six years later, a group of Pennsylvanians assaulted a surveyor hired by the Calverts to draw a line that apparently came a little too close to their farms.[14] Burgeoning populations in both colonies were the problem. Pennsylvania and Maryland had grown rapidly between 1680 and 1750. By midcentury, the population of the Upper South–Chesapeake region was rising faster than any other area except New England.[15] Maryland shared in this expansion, its population becoming as diverse as it was large.

No similar contention is possible regarding Maryland's economy, though; it remained fixated on tobacco, and with good reason. During the first half of the eighteenth century, the price per pound for Virginia and Maryland leaf either fell or remained flat, whereas British imports of tobacco rose dramatically.[16] Declining prices coupled with increased demand drove the region's cash-crop obsession to new heights. Of course, farmers still planted food crops, cereals and the like, and Maryland moved as quickly as any colony to exploit the growing hemispheric demand for American grain.[17] Tobacco, however, remained the colony's signature export, and competition for land on which to grow it became fierce. Meanwhile in Pennsylvania, the overall population skyrocketed between 1700 and 1750, rising from 18,000 to 119,700 inhabitants.[18] Immigrants poured into Penn's rapidly maturing colony, drawn by low land prices and the dream of becoming respectable yeoman farmers. Unlike their counterparts in Maryland, however, these men planned to grow crops for local and regional consumption, and only secondarily for export. Thus, small farms worked by free hands became the rule in Pennsylvania, attested to by the fact that the number of blacks in its total population remained stable, as it did throughout the Middle Atlantic, whereas it more than doubled in the Upper South.[19] By 1750, black slaves made up nearly one-third of Maryland's population, most of these men and women working on tobacco plantations.[20]

As Pennsylvania and Maryland matured, they tussled endlessly over land distribution, conflicts worsened by the absence of a clear border between the colonies. The heirs of Penn and Calvert, frantic for a settlement, moved to the courts for arbitration in 1750. Unfortunately, the judges only made matters worse. Although establishing a portion of the actual border itself, the court left the job of surveying the remainder up to the proprietary governments, working through commissioners set up to define the boundary in full. For the next 13 years, commissions came and went, as did the survey teams they hired, without a definitive settlement. As Pennsylvania and Maryland struggled to draw a line between themselves, violence continued to plague the countryside, especially in frontier areas. Claims and counterclaims routinely provoked confrontations between farmers. A series of imperial wars that pitted Britain against France only added to the colonies' woes. Disorganization tempted Indians allied with the French to strike at exposed towns and villages, and they did so with ferocious abandon. Safety, security, and peace of mind seemed as remote as ever.

By 1763, long after religion lost its centrality to the colonial enterprise in both places, Pennsylvania and Maryland shared a strip of disputed territory and little else. The border disagreement and the paralysis that characterized efforts to resolve it highlighted a process in which two distinct societies and cultures, indeed two identities, were emerging. Embryonic at this early date, these worlds nonetheless had begun to develop according to fundamentally divergent blueprints–one Northern, one Southern–defined primarily by economic assumptions and their associated social value systems. One area of conflict had to do with exactly who would do the labor required to make each colony thrive. Pennsylvanians wanted small farmers, craftspeople, and merchants; Maryland's planters turned increasingly to slaves.

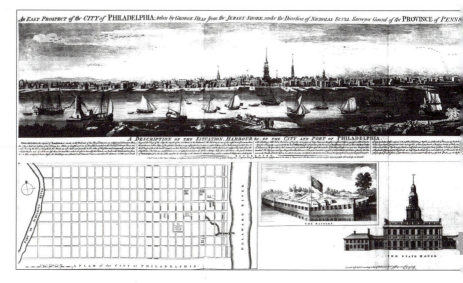

Pennsylvania was flourishing by the eighteenth century, and Philadelphia, seen here in this 1752 engraving, was its most active city. Philadelphia merchants gained wealth and power through the Atlantic trade, shipping goods to the West Indies, Europe, and beyond.

Pennsylvania in the eighteenth century was at the forefront of Northern commercialism. Agriculture in Pennsylvania, as in every colony, dominated the economic outlook of the common people, and subsistence farming remained common in many places. One observer noted that "in general the province is inhabited by small freeholders ... and many little ones who have the necessaries of life and nothing more."[21] Still, trade and commerce occupied a special place in Pennsylvania. Philadelphia, in particular, hummed with commercial activity. A visitor to the city in 1760 remarked that it was "in a very flourishing state, and inhabited by merchants, artists, tradesmen, and persons of all occupations." He wondered whether there could be "a greater pleasure ... Than in perceiving a rich and opulent state arising out of a small settlement or colony" such as Pennsylvania.[22] Philadelphia's merchants grew wealthy and powerful on an Atlantic trade that funneled large quantities of the colony's produce to the West Indies and beyond. By mid-century, Philadelphians routinely bequeathed estates approaching $400,000, in modern dollars, to the heirs. Some left inheritances of close to one million dollars.[23] This mercantile elite came to predominate in politics, and their interests slowly became those of Pennsylvania as a whole. Focused on multiple and varied markets, the merchant class helped Pennsylvania build a recognizably modern economy and a modern social structure to support it. The merchants encouraged light industry and manufacturing, and pursued a brand of commercial capitalism that fostered a complex social hierarchy within which social mobility and innovation were rewarded. Noting this arrangement, the political historian Richard Hofstadter commented that Pennsylvania's "repeated bursts of self-satisfaction ... seem on the whole to have been warranted."[24] Along with Boston and New York, Philadelphia was an unmistakably Northern city—with it went the rest of Pennsylvania.

Maryland took an altogether different course that would bestow upon it a Southern orientation and outlook. Like its northern neighbor, Maryland had bustling cities and a growing population. Annapolis continued to be the center of political attention, while Baltimore had grown from a sleepy village to a city of roughly 600 residents. The total population of Maryland pushed upward to over 141,000 by 1750.[25] Neither of the colony's premier cities, however, came anywhere close to matching Philadelphia's population of almost 30,000, nor could they compete with its bustling mercantile activity. Baltimore and Annapolis paled in terms of wealth and commercial enterprise. Philadelphia was larger, busier, and simply more important for one reason: Tobacco dominated neither the city's warehouses and wharves nor the productive energy of the colony's people.

Rather than being populated by farmers, craftspeople, and merchants mingling in a diversified, dynamic economy, Maryland wagered its future on barrels filled with tobacco leaves. Maryland was transfixed by the profit potential of tobacco. Like that of Virginia, the colony's economy revolved around the plant's cultivation, processing, and sale. Farms and plantations, therefore, rather than cities, dominated trade and directed Maryland's economic development and social structure. A highly localized, tightly focused economy demanded stability and regularity. Change, innovation, and social mobility were, therefore, far less prized in Maryland than in Pennsylvania. In fact, perhaps

## THE YOKE OF TOBACCO

Tobacco dominated the society and culture of the Chesapeake from its earliest days until the American Revolution. Although other crops were grown and other commodities traded, tobacco remained central to the region's economy for over 100 years. Around this cash crop, an entire social structure and complex symbolic network grew and flourished. Tobacco was the primary determinant of where one stood in relation to others. Control of the tobacco crop and its market gave one effective control over the social order. Growing and selling this leafy product, however, regulated affairs horizontally within the elite as much as vertically between the various classes. Planters shipped their crops each year before the final sale price in the London trading houses had been set or the strength of the market for that year even known. Once the tobacco ships left port, months, if not longer, could pass before planters found out how well their crop had fared and how much, if any, profit would be realized from its sale. Debt, therefore, became a core element in Tidewater society and culture because planters basically wagered on future price levels and made current purchases on credit. Purchases of imported or luxury goods were generally made directly from tobacco traders known as "factors," who routinely extended credit to growers in Virginia and Maryland. Day-to-day expenses, however, had to be covered through borrowing from one's neighbors. Webs of lending and owing resulted, therefore, that spanned plantation fields across the Tidewater region, leading to a system of elite relations in which honor and integrity were inextricably bound up with debt, and debt with tobacco. One of these indebted planters became the third president of the United States—Thomas Jefferson. Indeed, Jefferson once became so ensnared in debt that he was forced to plead with a British merchant to help him out of a situation in which he became involved financially with a less-than-reliable fellow planter. "I must beg you," Jefferson wrote, "to have me secured ... Should my friend prove unsuccessful ... I might sweep away the whole of my little fortune."* The future president feared tobacco-driven debt and died in it.

*T. H. Breen, *Tobacco Culture: The Mentality of the Great Planters on the Eve of Revolution* (Princeton, N.J.: Princeton University Press, 1985), 144.

no better contrast to Pennsylvania's emergent modern order can be found than Maryland's traditional socioeconomic structure.

A countryside dominated by wealthy planters who manipulated the local economy for their own benefit seemed more appropriate to the Middle Ages than the Enlightenment. "The tobacco planters," wrote one commentator, "live more like country gentlemen of fortune than any other settlers in America."[26] Small farmers subordinated to this planter elite resembled medieval manor serfs more than enterprising yeoman freeholders. Indeed, Maryland's simple hierarchy harmonized with the colony's single-minded pursuit of tobacco profits. The historian T. H. Breen has summed up the matter by arguing that for people in Maryland, as in Virginia, tobacco created a unique and durable identity: "Tobacco shaped their society and helped define their place in it ... By 1750, this staple had been tightly woven into the fabric of the colonists' everyday life; it gave meaning to their experience."[27] In this respect, Maryland fell right in line with the rest of the colonial South. Nowhere from Calvert's colony to Georgia would one find the economic dynamism and social fluidity that had begun to develop in the colonial North by the mid–eighteenth century. Similarly, nowhere in the North would one find an entire social, cultural, and economic edifice, like that of Maryland and the other Southern colonies, supported by an ancient system of labor—slavery.

American racial slavery evolved from a practice known as indentured servitude. Colonial America suffered from severe labor shortages throughout its early history. To fill this need, colonists offered land to young men in exchange for a set period during which their labor would belong to someone else. In brief, colonial planters promised a parcel of land, and the means to work it, to any men who were willing to sell themselves into servitude, usually for a period of seven years. The system was designed to meet the need for unskilled labor while increasing the white English population of America. Indentured servitude, however, turned out to be an unwieldy and unreliable system. A steady flow of labor, for one thing, was never guaranteed, and retention of that labor over time was an impossibility built into the system itself, namely, the set duration of bound service. It proved to be expensive as well, once the initial cost of the indenture, maintenance of the servant, and the price of the final release were factored in. Slavery offered an attractive alternative.

Black slaves arrived in America rather inauspiciously in 1619, as the cargo of a Dutch ship that put in at Jamestown. For a time, slaves were treated mostly as bond servants; however, that condition did not last, for a series of laws soon transformed black servants into slaves. By the 1680s, chattel slavery, a system whereby black slaves inherited the status of being the lifelong property of their masters, had effectively replaced white indentured servitude throughout the South. Several developments account for this change. To begin with, as Southern cash-crop economies expanded, the need for unskilled gang labor grew. Planters needed ever greater numbers of strong backs. Because of the sheer size of any such labor force, cost became more of an issue. A work force made up entirely of indentured servants, in this sense, would have been prohibitively expensive. Slaves, on the other hand, provided a low-cost option. On average, it cost $390 to $650 (in modern figures) to cover an indentured servant's transportation from England; a slave could be shipped from Africa or the West Indies for between $193 and $260. The average purchase price for servants was $780; slaves could be bought for $612.[28] Better still, from the planters' point of view, slaves and their offspring could be held in bondage for their entire natural lives. The end of indenture payout required by the contracts of white servants would not apply to black slaves. Virginia tobacco planters, for example, could keep the "ten bushels of Indian corn, thirty shillings in money ... and one well fixed musket ... of the value of twenty shillings at least" that a 1705 law demanded they give to indentured servants upon release.[29]

The use of slave labor did more than increase the planters' profit margins. Slaves functioned as a degraded, powerless foundation that supported and stabilized the white Southern social order. Their position on the very bottom rung of society's ladder provided a racial buffer that quieted poor white discontent while insulating the planter elite against challenges to their dominance. Slaves served as a permanent underclass that assured poor whites of at least a modicum of respect and dignity. No matter how bad matters became, those in the lower class could comfort themselves with the fact that they would never slip any lower; come what may, they would never be black. Slavery thus reinforced the existing social hierarchy and neutralized class conflict, while providing an inexpensive, reliable source of laborers who could be worked as long and as hard as the master chose. In the words of Edmund Morgan, slavery both proved profitable and helped to "separate dangerous free whites from dangerous slave blacks by a screen of racial contempt."[30] It stood out as a system perfectly matched to the traditional, hierarchical, cash-crop economy and society that had begun to develop in Maryland and throughout the South.

This is not to say that indentured servitude or slavery was absent in the North. Slaves could be found in sizable numbers in New York and Rhode Island, not to mention Pennsylvania. Slavery, though, never occupied the central socioeconomic place in the North, particularly Pennsylvania, that it did in Maryland. Pennsylvania's economy, for one thing, was too diverse and too well balanced to need or depend on a slave labor force. Slavery offered no benefit to a commercially oriented people whose business interests shifted with the market. The social hierarchy was too fluid and the barriers to social mobility too easily overcome to have much use for the class stabilization guaranteed by a perpetually degraded underclass. Finally, the Quaker legacy of equality among God's children opposed the central assumptions on which slavery was based. The Quaker community never accepted slavery on Southern terms and quickly assumed a leadership position in the abolitionist movement. Free labor, performed by free people, would become the rule in Penn's colony. On this count, as on many others, Pennsylvania and Maryland could not have been more different. This contrast is reflected in the number of blacks, mostly slaves, in the populations of both colonies. In 1740, almost 21 percent of the population in Maryland was black, 40 years later, it would stand at nearly 33 percent. During this same period, the number remained stable in Pennsylvania, at a mere 2.4 percent.[31]

Through the late seventeenth and early eighteenth centuries, two separate cultures and societies emerged in the Chesapeake region. Two orders based on different ideas about the nature and direction of social and economic progress faced each other across an as yet ill defined boundary. The American colonies had begun to polarize toward either the commercial, soon-to-be industrial North or the staple-based agricultural slave South. Nowhere was this felt more keenly than along the margin where the two worlds shouldered up against one another. If not yet on the map, lines were already being drawn in people's minds.

**4**

# The Surveyors

The men chosen to settle, once and for all, the boundary dispute between Pennsylvania and Maryland shared a passion for measurement, whether in the sky or on the ground, and an inclination for adventure. Charles Mason and Jeremiah Dixon welcomed the challenge of resolving the argument in America, but for very British reasons. Neither man really had the slightest idea what the line they were to draw would mean to the Americans separated by it. Indeed, neither Mason nor Dixon grasped the true significance of the boundary they would craft, one border set down in an obscure corner of the vast eighteenth-century British Empire.

Charles Mason and Jeremiah Dixon were the two scientists chosen in 1763 to establish a true border between Pennsylvania and Maryland and settle the boundary dispute between the two colonies. The men welcomed the challenge, but neither man understood the significance of the border they would create or its effect on the colonies in the coming decades.

Charles Mason, the senior member of the duo, perhaps the more mature and certainly the better scientist, clearly felt the Enlightenment impulse to explore. Edwin Danson has labeled Mason "an adventurer, a man of his time," with an "eye for a fine line" and a "deep love of geometric form."[32] Like so many young men of his generation, Mason regarded setting up imperial boundaries as a purely scientific, mathematical exercise. The local impact of that exercise mattered far less than the challenge of bringing European-style order to a faraway land. As would become common later in Africa, European empires drew lines all over the world without much thought as to what exactly was being delineated and defined by their pens. As a result, their efforts guaranteed bitter disagreements and violent clashes among the local populations subjected to this brand of imperial arrogance. While the imperial center flattered itself that problems were being solved, the colonial periphery watched as its unique difficulties were given a new face but never actually worked out. The European royal courts unwittingly aggravated problems and amplified differences rooted in the novel circumstances of colonial development. The imperial center-periphery relationship was often plagued by difficulties that were only "partially grasped but by no means fully defined and certainly not resolved to the mutual satisfaction of all concerned parties."[33]

Charles Mason acted out one small role in this drama of misperception. In the broadest sense, he served as an instrument every bit as precise and dutiful as the surveying tools he manipulated. Mason, in fact, operated as an agent of imperial order whose impact on the American future exceeded anything the English astronomer could have anticipated. Born in 1728, in the village of Oakridge Lynch, Gloucestershire, Mason was a typical product of the English countryside. One of four children born to a rural baker, Mason probably would have followed in his father's footsteps had it not been his good fortune to have a benefactor; a mathematician from a neighboring hamlet paid for him to attend grammar school. It was at the Tetbury School that Mason's love of numbers and skill at calculation were first noticed. These qualities put him on track for a career in science. By the time he was 28 years old, Mason had accepted a position as an assistant astronomer at the famous Greenwich Observatory. There, he earned a modest salary that allowed him to marry and start a family. His real love remained mathematics, though, and he reveled in his work at Greenwich. Only within its walls could he spend his time gazing into the heavens, imagining all the lines that connected the tiny points of light he saw.

Mason demonstrated an uncanny ability to visualize and superimpose boundaries where none existed in nature. He also revealed an obsession with recordkeeping. A patient and careful

## LIFE AFTER THE SURVEY

Charles Mason spent the year after his departure from America engaged in even more extensive astronomical studies and striving to budget his income from the Pennsylvania-Maryland survey. In 1769, Mason observed and recorded a second transit of Venus, and he marveled at the appearance of the same comet that auspiciously marked the birth of the future French emperor, Napoleon Bonaparte. The astronomer's next great accomplishment was a personal one. Mason's first marriage had ended with the death of his beloved wife, Rebekah, in 1759. Alone for 11 years, he finally remarried in 1770, setting up a home with Mary Williams, the daughter of a close friend. Mason studied and surveyed for 17 years before returning to America in 1786. Bringing his family with him this time, Mason corresponded with Benjamin Franklin before falling ill and dying in Philadelphia on October 25, 1786. Jeremiah Dixon never looked back at America. Always in search of adventure, Dixon returned to England only to team up with Mason one last time for the Venus observations. After parting again, Dixon traveled to Norway before retiring to County Durham. Settling down as something of a country gentleman did not translate into sitting still. The ever-active Dixon surveyed local estates and laid out fields; he drew maps and worked with Parliament, while becoming wealthier than he ever imagined. The high point of his professional life came in 1773, when he was elected to the Royal Society. Five years later, Dixon died at age 45, never having married but having lived a full life. He was buried in a nearby Quaker cemetery.

man, Mason compulsively organized numbers and lost himself in tabulation. He recorded everything, laboring to squeeze the world into tidy columns and reorder it as sensible equations rendering sensible solutions. Mason's character suited him well for service in the close confines of a chilly observatory. It also gave him the skills for visualizing lines crisscrossing real and imagined landscapes. Mason liked a good math problem, but his vision never transcended the angles, degrees, numbers, and formulas with which he worked. America would be simply one more mathematical challenge, one more puzzle to solve. Its people, culture, societies, and future did not figure into his calculations. The line he would help draw between two distant colonial outposts meant more to him than the places it would separate. Mason stood on the fringes as a dispassionate imperial observer. He had little, if any, desire to understand the place where his name would become synonymous with the division between North and South.

Jeremiah Dixon lost even less sleep over the America he would partition than did his senior partner. Mason, once in North America, at least took notice of the natural world around him and commented on the people he met; Dixon could not have cared less. The colonies and their conflicts, tensions, and disputes meant next to nothing to him. Working with Mason merely meant a job, and a fairly good one at that, given the handsome paycheck the team would be offered to adjudicate the Penn-Calvert case. Five years Mason's junior, Dixon was born in County Durham, England, in July 1733. He was one of eight children whose father, a devout Quaker, operated a coal mine. Dixon's religious affiliation should have given him an edge in Quaker-dominated Pennsylvania, but like so much else in his life, Dixon never had the patience to pursue a life of faith; long before reaching America, he had become a Quaker in name only. Dixon went to school at a small rural academy and, like Mason, proved to be something of a prodigy in mathematics. Being a natural with numbers, Dixon taught himself astronomy and took a series of jobs assisting more-established scientists. He eventually made enough of a name to be considered by the Royal Society as Mason's assistant on an expedition to Indonesia in 1761 to observe and record the transit of Venus, or the movement of the planet across the meridian. Assisting the better-known Mason in the study of a rare astronomical event boosted Dixon's reputation and gave him the opportunity to demonstrate his competence as an astronomer and a surveyor. Dixon saw only opportunity in his instructions "to accompany Mr Mason and be under his directions"[34] on the trip to Indonesia, as he would in a similar order to help Mason on the Pennsylvania-Maryland border in America. Dixon's partnership with Mason served as a convenient way for the aspiring scientist to establish himself in a respectable and growing field, that of geodetic survey, and earn a decent salary for the first time in his life. The little bit of adventure thrown in only sweetened the deal. Travel, career, money, and challenge motivated Mason and Dixon. In this, they resembled so many other imperial outsiders whose hands helped shape the contours of distant lands around the world.

At no point did imperial mapmakers consider the character of the places they divided and defined. With regard to America, the British government sought stability and peace above all other considerations. It did not relish the notion of elite proprietors squabbling in law courts while their people quarreled in a more violent manner. The dispute between Pennsylvania and Maryland compromised, however slightly, the economic development of each colony. Disorder made the Indian frontier less secure and thus less attractive to new immigrants whose labor would contribute to the enrichment of the empire as a whole. Turmoil cut into profits and reduced revenue. Political instability affected trade. The imperial economy, so the thinking went, was a delicately balanced system of interconnected regional and local economies; trouble in one sector, therefore, soon spread to others. The royal administration worried that even the smallest difficulty, such as an inability to define a provincial border, might compromise economic development and hinder progress regionally, with reverberations in Britain. Social and cultural peculiarities on a local level might be of interest to scholars, but the imperial administrators in London cared far more about trade figures and revenue tallies.

Thus, the dispute between the Penns and Calverts had to be settled. Maryland exported huge amounts of tobacco, and its plantations were inextricably tied to those in Virginia, creating a unified source of a precious and profitable commodity. Tobacco comprised three-quarters of the total exports leaving the Chesapeake.[35] The uncertainties associated with cultivation, processing, and shipment determined the relative health of a sizable portion of the imperial market. Pennsylvania, too, had acquired economic significance. It remained a commercial hub, but during the first half of the eighteenth century, it also became an important source of wheat throughout the Atlantic area. The colony's small farmers turned out immense quantities of cereal crops to satisfy the demands of a growing hemispheric population. As a result, wheat prices doubled between 1720 and 1770 as more of the colony's grain left Philadelphia bound for the West Indies and beyond.[36] Maryland and Pennsylvania might have been located on the fringes of the English world, but as far as the imperial economy was concerned, they represented key components. Keeping them orderly and at peace became a paramount issue.

A clear, mutually acknowledged border would end proprietary haggling, facilitate local development, and contribute to the profitability of colonial America, thus enriching England itself. Like Mason and Dixon, imperial officials did not give much thought to colonial social and cultural evolution. The government, in fact, viewed the American colonies as an undifferentiated provincial mass. That the colonial North and South, both English, might be moving in different directions did not occur to the men who sat in London overseeing the empire. The notion that two divergent cultures could be developing alongside one another was lost on officials who lumped together Pennsylvania trade goods and Maryland tobacco, who saw no difference between the former's yeoman farmers and independent craftspeople and the latter's planters and slaves. Much like the imperial surveyors themselves, the British government did not understand exactly what it was drawing a line between.

The two men who drew one of the most important borders in American history, as well as their employers, neither thought nor cared a great deal about the line's future significance. They could not know that their creation would become the first tiny, almost imperceptible, tear in the fabric of a nation that did not yet exist. Of course, neither Mason nor Dixon can be blamed for this. Their job description did not include trying to divine the course of American cultural history. Their journey to the British Empire's periphery, driven by personal and imperial motives, was a paying proposition having to do with geography, not politics or sociology. The men eagerly anticipated the opportunity to further their careers while experimenting with novel scientific instruments—nothing more. The entire exercise was designed to resolve a tiresome provincial quarrel that, in itself, was of only passing interest to the pair. Ironically, the map work would far surpass its creators in historical significance. Mason and Dixon would leave surnames stored away in the American memory; their line, however, would play a leading role in a drama that shaped America's history. That their creation was arbitrary took nothing away from its potential to affect lives and destinies on both sides of it. However imaginary or contrived the Mason-Dixon Line might have been, it possessed an unnatural power to alter the thoughts and actions of the people it divided.

# 5

# Drawing
# Imperial Lines

Mason and Dixon became celebrities after their successful voyage to record the transit of Venus in 1761. All London buzzed with news of the remarkable accomplishment, and their names found their way into conversations throughout the capital. As the subject of so much talk, the pair quickly drew the attention of the Penns and Calverts. Both sides in the Pennsylvania-Maryland dispute craved a settlement and needed men skilled at measurement to arrive at one. Years of angry recriminations and aborted survey attempts had proven to be exhausting distractions from the real business of making a go of it in America. The colonial proprietors had to have a final determination of the border between their holdings. Local surveyors seemed incapable of meeting the challenge, so the Penns and Calverts sought a recommendation from the Royal Observatory, which referred them to Mason and Dixon. After making the initial contacts, the proprietors put forward a generous offer: £600

Setting a boundary between their colonies was so important to the leaders of Pennsylvania and Maryland that they hired the most famous astronomer-mathematicians of the time, Mason and Dixon, and paid them generously. Mason and Dixon won acclaim after charting the transit of Venus in 1761. An artificial view of that transit in London is seen here in this 1769 print.

(around $60,000 today) for each man's work, plus expenses. Neither Mason nor Dixon was in a position to turn down such an attractive paycheck, so on August 4, 1763, the two astronomer-mathematicians signed a contract obliging them to establish a true border between Maryland and Pennsylvania. They sailed for America one month later.

The land Mason and Dixon would measure and divide was as rough-hewn as the cabins and farmhouses most of its inhabitants lived in. Despite extensive and growing urbanization, America remained something of a wild, wooded, though very valuable, frontier of the British Empire. Cities such as Boston, New York, Charleston, Baltimore, and Philadelphia already bustled with the type of activity one would find in any urban center. By the time Mason and Dixon sailed, Philadelphia alone had a population that had grown by 30 percent in just over 40 years to a total of nearly 24,000 residents.[37] Taken together, 73,000 colonial Americans lived in cities by the 1760s, close to 5 percent of the entire population of just over one and a half million people.[38] Still, 90 percent of all Americans lived in the countryside, in thousands of towns, villages, hamlets, plantations, and isolated farmsteads. It was here that one could see the real results of an astonishing 219 percent increase in the white population and an even larger rise in its black counterpart:[39] land disputes combined with soaring production of raw resources for the export market, accelerated westward migration, and the urgent need for the type of order and organization that successive imperial administrations had failed to provide. Great Britain had planted its colonies in the New World and enjoyed the products of its lands; now it would have to manage them.

Great Britain added to its own burden when, in 1763, it grafted Canada onto its American provinces. Eleven years of war against the French, in both North America and Europe, resulted in the British seizure of French Canada and the empire's ascension to supreme power on the continent. All this new land and all these new subjects required a more active administrative hand and clearer regulation of economic and political affairs.

The problem lay in the fact that this intensified intervention in colonial matters depended on the judgment of men sitting comfortably 3,000 miles from the people they governed. As new colonies took shape and older ones matured and bickered with each other over land, royal officials in London were compelled to draw lines on maps of places they had never seen and did not understand. Presuming to comprehend colonial interests and mind-sets, these men regarded the lines as fair and reasonable; yet in reality their arbitrarily drawn boundaries divided societies and cultures that had developed to the point where they were alien to imperial assumptions. Colonial authorities and their mapmakers, in this manner, conveyed to the British government a false impression that it was directing the evolution of its North American provinces. It looked so tidy on paper, with all the little colonies in their proper places. Actually, British control and influence in the patterns and course of American growth rarely extended beyond those pieces of paper covered over with imaginary borders.

Mason and Dixon, as imperial agents, were prime examples of Britain's inability to appreciate the world that the empire strove to categorize, compartmentalize, and ultimately rule. Although they marveled at the natural beauty and expanse of the American wilderness (Mason much more so than Dixon), neither surveyor truly fathomed the heterogeneous, conflict-ridden shores onto which they stepped when they disembarked at Philadelphia on November 15, 1763. They had come to settle an old dispute and draw a border; that was all. Such disputes, common wisdom informed the pair, had periodically rocked the colonies from New York to Georgia; never had they amounted to anything a well-drawn line could not remedy. This time, however, the contest had overtones that were far from local in scope. Pennsylvania and Maryland, even by the 1760s, were moving in different directions. A slow, incremental process of polarization was taking place along the exact boundary Mason and Dixon would formalize. Although yet unseen, two inherently antagonistic Americas had begun to emerge—one North, one South—

out of the crucible of social and economic development. Lines eventually defined these two Americas, but not yet. For the time being, the prevalent divisions in colonial America ran longitudinally along the fluid, permeable, and contested boundary between the English settlers and the Indians.

Since the earliest days of colonization, the English and Native Americans had recognized an unofficial western boundary between their societies. Running along a north–south axis, often conforming to the contours of major mountain ranges, the border separated cultures with vastly differing agendas and ambitions. The first attempt to codify this border in law came in the 1640s in Virginia when, after nearly 30 years of conflict and bloodshed, Governor William Berkeley established a line in the far west of his colony to separate English farmers and the Indians. Within a few decades, unfortunately, a new wave of violence washed away Berkeley's line during an intra-English power struggle known as Bacon's Rebellion. It appeared that any effort to craft a political boundary between the new and the old Americas would come to nothing, and no further attempts were made. Another surge of racial hostility 100 years later, however, prompted the imperial government to give an official dividing line another try.

The war with France ended in September 1763 with both powers exhausted and the British seeking to bring order and peace to North America as quickly as possible. Their hopes dissolved in a violent Indian uprising in western Pennsylvania and Maryland. Led by an Ottawa warrior named Pontiac, Indian war parties attacked British outposts and settlements throughout the backcountry. Alarmed by the extent of the fighting and determined not to pour any further money or troops into America, the royal authorities in London drew a line down the crest of the Appalachian Mountains and proclaimed it, in November 1763, to be a secure, defined border with the Indian nations to its west. As the Proclamation of 1763 itself pointed out, the line would promote peaceful coexistence. War, especially the brutal frontier type common to America, undermined normal life, disrupted politics, and hindered trade. The crown, therefore, thought it "essential to our Interest, and the Security of our Colonies" for Indians and English to live in physically and legally separate worlds. Of course, with typical ambiguity, the Proclamation defined the Indian lands it set aside as "lying to the Westward of the Sources of the Rivers which fall into the Sea from the West and North West." [40]

The Proclamation of 1763 drew a line of demarcation that even people at the time viewed as arbitrary and, worse yet, illusory. Much as the imperial government conceived of the colonies as an undifferentiated whole, so it thought of the Indians as one big bloc set neatly to the west of the Appalachians. The reality was far more complex and dangerous. Americans, both Native and English, took this reality for granted. The historian Gary Nash, in fact, argues in no uncertain terms that the Proclamation Line "existed only on paper, and nobody, neither colonists nor Indians, took it seriously."[41] Indian parties continued to raid western settlements, and colonists persisted in their efforts to grab fertile land at Indian expense. The borderline settled nothing and only acted to amplify and accentuate differences between the contesting groups. It came to symbolize hostility between different cultures more than the peaceful separation of lives and goals. Like the one Mason and Dixon drew a few years later, the Proclamation Line, by highlighting rather than blurring distinctions, was a line begging to be crossed.

Mason and Dixon were keenly aware of the problems that required the royal proclamation of racial division along the Appalachians. In December 1763, violence flared on the frontier, just as the pair finished erecting an observatory in Philadelphia. The Cedar Street observatory afforded Mason and Dixon the opportunity to establish an astronomical reference point for their calculations of the precise location of the Pennsylvania-Maryland border. Its construction had no sooner been completed than news reached the city of fighting in the mountain foothills. Western Pennsylvania farmers, irked by the constraints of the Proclamation, cut off from the rich farmlands of the trans-Appalachian West, and hemmed into an ever-shrinking English area of settlement, lashed out at local Indians. Seething with anger and resentment, a band of farmers attacked a village belonging to the peaceful Conestoga tribe and slaughtered its inhabitants. Some in Philadelphia publicly condemned the assault as wholesale murder; others condoned it as just retribution for Pontiac's raids earlier in the year. Everyone, however,

## PEACE BY PROCLAMATION

The Proclamation Line of 1763 became famous for its fluidity and as an irritant to Western farmers. The line never succeeded in keeping settlers and Indians apart, let alone guaranteeing a peaceful coexistence between the groups. The historian Robert Middlekauff put this failure in blunt terms when he argued that the Proclamation of 1763 did nothing to make the frontier more secure and that, in fact, "the West proved virtually ungovernable."* Indian raiding and trading parties routinely crossed into colonial areas, whereas farmers determined to exploit the rich soil of the trans-Appalachian West streamed through the mountain passes, setting up farmsteads and towns on the other side. The most famous of these trespassers was the legendary Daniel Boone. In complete disregard for the law, Boone led the way as settlers took up residence on Indian land in what would become the state of Kentucky. Useless in its separating function, the line quickly came to embody the type of imperial ignorance and arrogance that enraged Americans. Colonial polemicists railed against the presence of soldiers among them. When several British regiments from Canada arrived by ship in the city of Boston in 1768 to quell anti-British disturbances, the troops were viewed as an unwelcome extension of British power from the frontier into the heart of colonial America. With the sea on one side and the line on the other, both now patrolled by the British military, conspiracy-minded Americans came to the conclusion that a sinister plot had been hatched to imprison them. The soldiers, apparently viewed as representatives of the colonies' jailers, quickly became the focus of violent local resentment that boiled over into the Boston Massacre, the opening act of the American Revolution. The Proclamation Line thus proved to be a signal failure in just about every respect and, like the Mason-Dixon Line, caused more problems in the end than it solved.

*Robert Middlekauff, *The Glorious Cause: The American Revolution, 1763–1789* (New York: Oxford University Press, 1982), 148.

knew what it meant: Arbitrary lines drawn between hostile cultures inevitably provoked more violence than they prevented.

Such an understanding eluded imperial outsiders like Mason and Dixon, if Charles Mason's comments after a visit to the massacre site are to be trusted. During a stop at the location in January 1764, Mason mourned the loss of life and denounced "the Horrid and inhuman murder of 26 Indians, Men, Women, and Children, leaving none alive to tell."[42] Mason's thoughts at the wrecked village reveal a man unable to comprehend how such tragedies could occur given the fact that a clear boundary separated the English assailants from their Indian victims. The Proclamation of 1763 should have put an end to hatreds and suspicions that lay at the root of frontier violence. What Mason, an imperial agent, missed was the meaning of sociocultural borders to Americans. The division of land implied the apportionment of wealth and resources—hence, political power. The contenders subsequently polarized into exclusive blocs. Separate spheres emerged in which essentially economic concerns mutated into conflicting worldviews. These then hardened into mutual distrust and eventually resulted in bloodshed. Lines portended conflict, not coexistence.

Chalking up the Conestoga massacre to simple-minded colonial savagery, Mason and Dixon began work in early 1764. First, they established an eastern anchor for their survey by drawing a semicircular line around New Castle, Delaware, as stipulated in William Penn's original charter. This became the border between Pennsylvania and Delaware, which had separated from the former in 1701, and, when extended southward as the Tangent Line, the boundary separating Maryland and Delaware. An arduous task involving complex calculations and precise measurements, establishing the New Castle arc occupied the surveyors for most of 1764. By November of that year, with the Tangent Line and semicircle set, Mason and Dixon began to determine, using marker chains and charts, the West Line that would run from a post at the intersection of the Tangent and the semicircle toward the western mountains. Work on this portion of the border began in earnest in March 1765, with Mason keeping a meticulous journal containing details of the survey process and occasional commentary on the pair's travels across one small part of British America. Of passing interest to Mason, as he scribbled away, were locations such as the little stream they "crossed ... running into Antietam."[43] To Mason, the creek was rather unremarkable; it was just another obstacle to be overcome along the survey line. Ninety-seven years later, however, it would run red with the blood of soldiers, some fighting to cross the line Mason and Dixon were drawing, others desperately trying to repel them. The Civil War battle of Antietam in September 1862 would be the single bloodiest day of combat in American military history. For Mason, the crossing of Antietam Creek proved only slightly more worthy of note than the team's earlier fording of Marsh Creek, six miles south of a place that would later be called Gettysburg. There, in 1863, tens of thousands of Americans would die for causes defined and set in motion by the Mason-Dixon Line.

By the end of their first real year of work, the survey team had established the border between Pennsylvania and Maryland for a distance of 50 miles and had planted pillar-like stone markers to identify it. The pair then returned to Philadelphia just in time for the Stamp Act riots, which protested British taxation without American representation. Uncomfortable with the tumult and offended by the city's loose morals, Mason left by himself to tour the Chesapeake. Dixon, bachelor and thrillseeker that he was, remained to enjoy all of the commotion. Mason's travels took him into Virginia and then back again to Maryland. During a stop at the aptly named Port Tobacco, Mason caught a glimpse of the dark underside of colonial life, and the subject of the coming American debate between the North and the South. After breakfast one morning, Mason strolled down to the waterside and soon found himself in a crowd gathered around a ship just in from the West African coast. There he witnessed the auctioning of human beings, stolen from their homes, terrorized, and traumatized. Human beings, yes, but to the crowd swirling around Mason they were nothing more than a "Cargo of choice healthy SLAVES."[44] This was Maryland's disgrace as well as that of the South; it would be the future cause of an American tragedy.

After their break, Mason and Dixon pushed westward, marking the border as they went. At last, they reached a point in the western mountains past which the team's Indian guide refused to continue. They had stumbled upon a warpath used by local Indian villages; crossing it would invite attack. The surveyors then turned back, declaring their job done and the border set. The final map bearing the line they drew was delivered to representatives of Pennsylvania and Maryland in January 1768. In September of that year, Charles Mason and Jeremiah Dixon departed for England, but not before being recognized for their accomplishment and admitted as members of Philadelphia's American Society for Promoting Useful Knowledge. Mason would return to visit in 1786, with his family, and die in Philadelphia. Dixon would never see America again; he would die in County Durham in 1779.

In its form and function, the line Mason and Dixon left behind resembled any number of similar imperial boundaries drawn across eastern North America. Measured and recorded with the utmost precision, the Mason-Dixon Line, as far as the British and colonists at the time were concerned, simply delineated the border between two middling provinces of the mighty and vast British Empire. To Americans it would come to mean much more. The line would serve as a reference point for two divergent realities. It would separate two different models of American development that grew steadily more defined and sharply contrasted in the decades to come.

# 6

# The Border from the Revolution to the Missouri Compromise

Mason and Dixon returned to an imperial center that was slowly losing its grip on the colonial periphery. An empire that spanned the Atlantic began to dissolve in revolution. For decades, perhaps longer, the American provinces and the British parent country had been drifting apart. Americans chafed under the weight of trade regulations perceived to be unfairly restrictive. The British parliament refused to acknowledge 100 years of political evolution that had led the colonists to view, as the only legitimate authority over them, the provincial assemblies and houses of representatives located on their own soil. Taxation, always a subject of debate among legal theorists, became an issue when it came time to pay for the recently concluded war with France. By the 1770s, all of these factors became points of contention and were bitterly divisive. Within the American sphere, however, an even more wrenching split had opened, this one between those who envisioned the hand of liberty extended to all Americans and those who understood freedom to mean the ability to hold other people in chains. A preliminary match began between the opponents and supporters of slavery. Essentially a philosophical exchange at this point, the contest over slavery would take shape geographically as a polarization between an American North and an American South, glaring at one another across the Mason-Dixon Line.

The hardening of a simple colonial boundary into an ideological border began in 1780. That year, Pennsylvania assumed its position in the vanguard of liberty: The new state abolished slavery. Pennsylvania had been a hotbed of radical activity during the 1770s, and its citizens prided themselves on their revolutionary credentials. Their abolition of slavery represented a concrete attempt to realize the goals and dreams of the rebellion; it signified the fulfillment of the promise of liberty. Abolition also put Pennsylvania in the company of Massachusetts, which ended slavery the same year, and other Northern states either actively engaged in or moving toward abolition, each and every one of them located above the Mason-Dixon Line. Granted, Pennsylvania abolished slavery via a mechanism known as

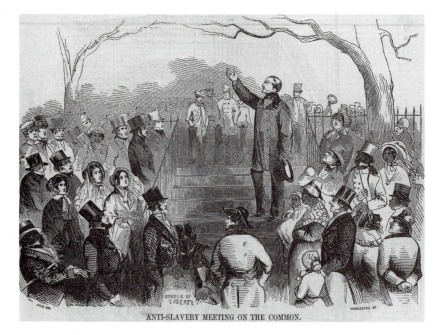

ANTI-SLAVERY MEETING ON THE COMMON.

The Mason-Dixon Line began to take on ideological significance in the late eighteenth-century. While Pennsylvania and states to its north introduced legislation for the abolition of slavery, Maryland sided with the Southern states in defending slavery. The line only gained importance in the nineteenth-century as the anti-slavery movement spread with rallies and speeches, like this one in Boston in 1851.

gradual emancipation; the institution would die out slowly over a period of years as all blacks born after 1780 were deemed free. But the state's laws of 1780 and a companion act of 1788, in the words of one scholar, "continued to be the most forceful anti-slavery statutes in the United States until the 1840s."[45] Except for New England, nowhere else was sentiment against slavery as strong as in Pennsylvania. Gary Nash and Jean Soderlund summed up the situation by arguing that "south of New England, slavery died first in Pennsylvania and it died there the fastest."[46]

Just below the Mason-Dixon Line lay a tier of states that did not accept the revolutionary notion that democracy was inconsistent with the institution of slavery. The Southern states nodded to liberty but held their property rights, in this case human property, to be sacred. Over the course of a century and a half, slavery had evolved by the late eighteenth century from an economic expedient to a core element of Southern life and thought; any challenge to its structural integrity or its philosophical foundations threatened the very essence of what it meant to be Southern. This was as true in Maryland as anywhere else in the South. Although some Marylanders had swung over to the side of abolition during the Revolution and had begun to agitate for change, most remained steadfastly against freedom for slaves. Pennsylvania was passing laws to guarantee liberty to its black community, but Maryland authorities refused even to consider liberty on an individual basis, known as manumission. In 1785, for example, the Maryland House of Delegates turned down a number of manumission petitions without consideration.[47] The petitions, interestingly, were generated under the guidance of a Maryland Quaker organization closely related to those of Pennsylvania. Forming themselves into an abolition society in 1791, the group annually petitioned the Maryland assembly to release slaves, to no avail. Maryland held fast to its citizens' rights when it came to owning other human beings. Ardent proslavery members of the House of Delegates went so far as to denounce abolitionism and any organization proposing it as "repugnant to the laws and constitution of [Maryland].[48] Although the positions reflected in the opposite courses being followed in Pennsylvania and Maryland had not yet jelled, a discernible tension between North and South could already be felt.

The fledgling United States at last secured its independence in 1783. Although its imperial troubles were now over, serious domestic problems abounded, chief among them the increasingly bitter debate over slavery. The dispute turned on one key issue: As the new republic matured socially and grew physically, what kind of nation would it be? Americans asked themselves whether the country could embrace both freedom and slavery at once and everywhere. If not, if two separate American realities were expected to coexist, some way of distinguishing them and marking them off from one another would have to be devised.

The peace settlement with Britain had resulted in the transfer of large tracts of land, reaching to the Mississippi River, into American hands. Eventually, this territory, much like the chunk of land that would be signed over to America by France in the Louisiana Purchase of 1803, would have to be divided and organized. Dividing it fairly between the rival camps—free and slave, North and South—would be tricky, if possible at all.

The first attempt at a solution took place in 1787. The Confederation Congress, predecessor to the Congress established by the Constitution, wrestled for years with the thorny problem of organizing the northwestern lands ceded to it by the British at the end of the Revolution. This territory, comprising the modern states of Ohio, Indiana, Illinois, Michigan, Wisconsin, and Minnesota, with its fertile farmland, seemed likely to fill up quickly and needed an organizational plan. The Northwest Ordinance served that purpose. The Ordinance divided the new land into territories composed of townships along lines proposed two years earlier by Thomas Jefferson. It next provided for territorial administrations that could petition for statehood once their area reached a population of 60,000 people, and it guaranteed those people the protections and liberties of a republican form of government. Most importantly, the Northwest Ordinance prohibited slavery throughout the region, thus indelibly marking the entire tier of future states as free. Using the Ohio River as a natural boundary, the Northwest Ordinance did not cover territory added in the South. This satisfied Southerners who sought the expansion of slavery and Northerners who envisioned its eventual demise; in this, the Ordinance represented an early effort at compromise. Still, by recognizing any border at all, the Confederation Congress extended and elaborated on the concept that became associated with the Mason-Dixon Line: an intra-American boundary between Northern freedom and Southern slavery. A notion of separation began to grow, that of a national line of demarcation, essentially an extension of the Mason-Dixon Line to the Mississippi, with real political, social, and cultural consequences.

The historian Joyce Appleby has identified this moment as the point at which the "Mason-Dixon line ceased then to be the surveyors' boundary between Pennsylvania and Maryland and took on its symbolic reference to the division between freedom and slavery."[49] By 1800, quarreling Americans, began to develop an obsession with lines, lines of separation and compromise.

America grew with astonishing speed in the decades following independence. Between 1790 and 1820, the nation's physical landscape and material culture changed dramatically, and with them so went the society. The development, however, proved uneven and specific to one or the other section, North or South. Though still fundamentally agrarian, the Northern states found themselves caught in the swirl and storm of modernization. Northern cities swelled, becoming more diverse and sophisticated. Factories sprang up along Northern rivers, especially in New England, producing vast amounts of high-quality manufactured goods, principally textiles, shoes, clocks, firearms, and other consumer products. Along with the cities and factories came a new working class eager for a better life and demanding a louder political voice. A prosperous business class willing to exploit the workers' dreams and seeking a political order conducive to its interests also emerged. The new environment in the North fostered a mind-set oriented toward the future. New ways of thinking that prized innovation, social mobility, and change took hold. Northerners shared in a process in which, according to Richard D. Brown, "modernization of the economic structure promoted a more complete realization of the modern personality among Americans."[50] Little room was left in such a worldview for an archaic institution like slavery.

Change occurred in the South as well, though to a lesser degree and often in an opposite direction from that in the North. Part of the problem resulted from the industrialization sweeping the Northeastern states. Northern mills relied on Southern cotton to weave fabric, encouraging the South to retain its cash-crop economic focus. It also allowed a reactionary, almost feudal outlook to persist among Southerners. The invention of the cotton gin in 1793, a machine that made it easier to process raw cotton, and the opening of land in the Southwest to cultivation made this inertia profitable. Profit, in turn, convinced Southerners that their interests were best served by shoring up the plantation-based, slave-dependent economic foundation upon which their society and culture rested. For Southerners, change meant improving on but not moving away from tradition. Cities in the South grew, to be sure, along with trade and some light industry, but the region remained tethered to a cash-crop agricultural model defined by slavery. Unlike the dynamic, essentially modern society of the North, that of the South clung tenaciously to a rigidly hierarchical, static, traditional ideal that scorned modernity and embraced ideas and institutions, like slavery, whose day had passed.

As time went by, the core interests and agendas of these two societies ground against one another in many ways. For the most part hostile, the Northern and Southern societies interacted primarily through tacit agreements to leave each other alone, a series of fictitious "compromises" that actually settled very little and served mainly to avoid a clash over slavery. Compromise became a way in which North and South could pretend that slavery was not the divisive, defining issue everyone knew it was. Compromise was, in effect, a form of self-induced moral and political blindness that resulted in the carving of America into separate spheres of interest and activity. Through quiet agreement and unspoken contract, the relationship between North and South in the early nineteenth century came to depend on maintaining a balance in all matters between free and slave states, especially when it came to land and political representation. To guarantee each an equal say in the operation and destiny of the country, North and South had to be balanced in terms of the number of states in each bloc. Of course, the territory covered by the Northwest Ordinance would enter the Union in due time without slavery, but the Southwest would eventually do so with slavery; the trade seemed fair to all parties. Other new territories, however, were up for grabs. Sectional harmony hinged

Southerners fought fiercely in defense of slavery because it was such a significant part of their daily way of life. In this photograph from Atlanta during the Civil War, the slave auction house was located right in the center of town amidst the tobacco stores, markets, and other businesses.

on these areas. Bringing new states into the Union in tandem—one entering free for each that did so with slavery and vice versa—guaranteed a political stalemate of sorts, a reassurance to each side that neither had an excessive degree of power and influence. Talking about political apportionment allowed Americans to avoid a serious discussion of slavery by cloaking the issue in legislative euphemism, as states debated the equality of representation rather than the immorality of slave labor. Geography gave Americans the chance to delude themselves into believing that they could dodge the inevitable.

Unfortunately, the country was running out of space and time. Sectional tensions grew as the opponents and supporters of slavery found themselves in uncomfortable proximity. By 1819, at least one U.S. senator floated the idea of a line to separate and define how states were admitted and to which of the two sections they would give their allegiance. The suggestion generated little interest at the time, but most people in Washington knew that some similar measure would have to be adopted sooner or later. Influential politicians began to whisper about a border between slavery and freedom, an extension of the Mason-Dixon Line across the continent, if not in strict cartographical terms then certainly in spirit. Such a line might avert a national schism that could lead to civil war.

As Congress convened in 1820, a political crisis arose to test this theory. Missouri reached the population threshold for statehood. Missouri, however, had been settled mostly by slave holders who brought their human property with them. Lying almost in its entirety to the south of any theoretical extension of the Mason-Dixon Line, Missouri was destined to enter the Union as a slave state. To admit it as such, though, required creating exactly the geopolitical imbalance Americans feared. The initial bill for statehood thus proposed the abolition of slavery in the territory, but Southerners refused to see slavery extinguished from a place where it had been so firmly planted. Conflict loomed as the nation was forced to debate openly the geographical and political relationship between slavery and freedom.

Recognizing a potential showdown, the South demanded that Missouri be admitted as a slave state; Northerners countered with a demand for free-state status. Congress reached an impasse more quickly than anyone anticipated, an impasse that threatened to blow open a rift that had been carefully concealed since the colonial era. Kentucky's representative and Speaker of the House, Henry Clay, noted worriedly that some members of Congress were already murmuring about the existence of irreconcilable differences between North and South. Clay remarked that Missouri forced on Americans "a most unhappy question" that promised an unwelcome "awakening of sectional feelings." The Kentuckian summed up the mood, and danger, of the moment by claiming that the "words, civil war and disunion, are uttered almost without emotion."[51]

Clay worried that passions could rage out of control over Missouri. Working feverishly behind the scenes, he helped engineer a compromise based on the concept behind the Mason-Dixon Line: a clear delineation between competing Northern and Southern claims, agendas, and realities. Cooperating with other congressmen and some senators, Clay helped draft a plan whereby Missouri would enter the Union as a slave state in

## THE PROCESS OF COMPROMISE

Southern suspicion of Northern intentions in Missouri was not altogether unfounded. Although no conspiracy to destroy slavery ever existed, the New York congressman who sponsored Missouri's bid to enter the Union did seek to abolish slavery in the new state. Congressman James Tallmadge, Jr., submitted twin bills in 1819 for the admission of Missouri. One was the actual admission act in which Tallmadge included a clause prohibiting new residents from bringing slaves with them into the state. The second bill provided for the gradual emancipation of all slaves already in Missouri through a process in which slaves born after admission would be freed at age 25. Tallmadge drew on the experience of his native state in crafting his plan; New York had emancipated its slaves in a similar manner. The presumption that led Tallmadge to compare rough-and-tumble Missouri with venerable New York was that the former had fewer slaves than many places in the South, thus making it less Southern. He was wrong. Southern congressmen stood solidly against the Tallmadge amendments until one of their own stepped up to revise and push through the Missouri bills. Senator Jesse B. Thomas of Illinois took over the process and eventually shepherded Missouri statehood through Congress. Henry Clay provided the force behind Thomas's bid, and, like Thomas, understood what it meant to bring slavery as far North as Missouri supporters proposed. Clay was from the future border state of Kentucky. Thomas knew perhaps even a little bit more about slavery in a Southern state that bordered the North—Thomas was originally from Maryland.

exchange for Maine being admitted as a free state. The precious balance was maintained. The heart of the deal was a provision for drawing a line to avoid future confrontations. The Missouri Compromise laid out a line of demarcation that began at the Mason-Dixon and then followed the Ohio River to a point on the Mississippi River at latitude 36°30'. From there, the line ran officially to the edge of the Louisiana Territory, but theoretically it continued to the Pacific Coast. With the exception of Missouri itself, which formally entered the Union in 1821, any state above the Compromise Line that was added to the Union after 1820 would automatically become a free state, and any entering below the line would be a slave state. The line, therefore, divided and insulated two parts of the same country from each other. The Senate agreed and passed the compromise bills; the House of Representatives followed suit. The tide of intemperate language receded, and both sides took comfort in finally having a mutually recognized political and legal border between North and South.

The line as a tool of compromise was accepted into law and common practice. Once, a line drawn on a map did little more than vaguely suggest regional and cultural differences between colonial Pennsylvania and Maryland. Now it openly recognized the incompatibility of two halves of the same country. The line established by the Missouri Compromise was an extension but also an elaboration of the Mason-Dixon Line that delayed but could not prevent a final reckoning between North and South. Artificial though such lines were, they nonetheless embodied the growing tensions that already signified deep trouble for the nation. The two sections might not yet be at the point of divorce, but they were undeniably estranged.

# 7

# Erasing the Line
## The Crisis of the 1850s

The Missouri Compromise extended the Mason-Dixon Line physically and conceptually, applying its principle on a national scale. Like the Mason-Dixon Line, the 36°30' line provided Americans with a comforting sense of spatial division and the illusion of peaceful coexistence between mutually exclusive worldviews. Neatly separated in their own spheres, the two Americas occupied the same political space while following widely divergent developmental paths: one toward modernity and freedom, the other looping back on itself toward tradition and slavery. Going their own ways, the sections did their best to avoid discussion and debate. Still, periodic disputes tested the integrity of the Missouri Compromise and the very notion that such profound ideological and cultural tensions could be eased by an imaginary line drawn on a map.

Change accelerated rapidly in the first half of the nineteenth century but, once again, unevenly. Richard Brown has argued that while the North was "developing mechanized industry and agriculture, railroad transportation, long-distance communications, universal literacy, and an active citizenry," the South languished. In fact, according to Brown, "the slave states coalesced around a Southern ideal that reinforced their most traditional elements." This contrast resulted in a "growing tension between the eager modernization of the North and the incomplete, reluctant modernization of the South...."[52] By any measure, the North outpaced the South in the degree to which it embraced innovation and the rate in which it grew.

The United States as a whole became more crowded between the 1820s and the 1850s, but its cities fairly exploded during the decades prior to the Civil War. New York counted 515,000 people by 1850; Philadelphia swelled to 340,000.[53] Fueled by almost frantic industrialization, metropolises composed of core cities surrounded by smaller cities and towns mushroomed in the fertile soil of the North, as did the new cities to the west, such as Chicago, Cincinnati, and Pittsburgh. Pittsburgh moved out of the orbit of Philadelphia rather early and led the urban west in the rise of the recognizably modern

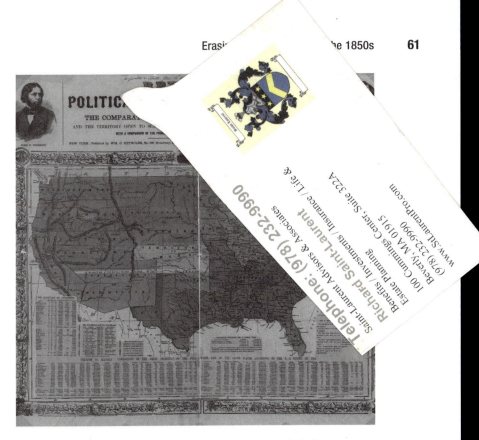

With the expansion of the United States came the question of whether new states would support abolition or be slave states. Henry Clay's solution in 1820 was the Missouri Compromise, which created a line separating the North and the South extending from the Mason-Dixon Line to the Mississippi River. This 1856 map of the United States displays the area of free states compared with that of slave states.

phenomenon known as suburbs. Indeed, the urban historian Richard Wade claims that the "centrifugal movement" of western cities spawning suburbs "was strongest in Pittsburgh."[54] Linked by telegraph, railroads, commerce, and finance, the North, east and west, pulsed with activity, all of it the result of free labor operating in a modern economy. Northerners took off and refused to look back.

The South, in contrast, inched forward, restrained by a traditional economy based on cotton and slavery. Below the Mason-Dixon Line, the world moved more slowly than in the North, drifting along a developmental path that looked backward at

almost every turn. Southern cities, for example, remained small
compared with their Northern counterparts. Despite its prime
location at the mouth of the Mississippi River, New Orleans
claimed only 132,000 people by the middle of the nineteenth
century; Baltimore had just a shade more at 169,000.[55] Other
Southern cities were even smaller, and none possessed the type
of industrial base that was becoming common in the North.
Urbanization moved at a crawl south of the Mason-Dixon Line.
Instead of acting as economic hubs, generating wealth and radiating power, Southern cities remained what they had always
been: supports for the *real* South of the cotton plantation.
Indeed, plantations dominated the South to the point where
they skewed the overall distribution of wealth. Unlike the balanced economy of the North, where city and country shared in
the prosperity, wealth in the South was disproportionately concentrated on cotton plantations. Maryland, in particular, which
one researcher noted was not considered technically "part of the
cotton South," experienced a distribution of wealth that identified the state as "definitely not representative of northern agriculture."[56] Slavery and a cash-crop focus tainted everything and
everyone in the South.

By 1850, cotton had literally become "king" in the American
South. The old Southwest, the area roughly between Georgia and
the Mississippi River, had been opened during the presidency of
Andrew Jackson in the 1830s. Known at times as the Black Belt
because of the richness of its soil, the land had belonged to the
Indians until the federal government forcibly removed them
from it in 1835–1837 and opened the region to planters from the
coastal South. Movement into the region was driven by the
growth of Northern textile mills; as mill operations expanded, a
lucrative market for processed cotton emerged. Southern
planters responded by buying millions of acres of land in places
like Mississippi and Alabama. As the planters moved in to cultivate the land and enrich themselves, they brought along their
slaves. Approximately 2.5 million slaves worked the land in the
American South by 1850, creating a permanent bond between

slavery and prosperity. Slavery was paramount to continued economic growth and more deeply embedded than ever in Southern society. Slavery, moreover, anchored Southern culture and produced a collective identity that regarded change and innovation with suspicion, if not as threats. Weighed down by cotton and slaves, the South looked toward a future identical to its past—and refused to budge.

Two distinct worlds, separated by vast cultural landscapes as well as the Mason-Dixon and Missouri Compromise lines, had hardened into position. Compromise thus became at once more important and less likely as time went on. Americans were still talking to one another but were less inclined to listen. The direction taken by future debates depended on how willing Americans were to respect the concept of boundaries, however fictitious or arbitrary. California offered the first real test of just how far both sides were willing to go.

The United States went to war with Mexico in 1846 largely to gain control of the western half of the continent, particularly California, which at the time possessed the finest natural harbor on the Pacific Coast, San Francisco. Propelled by the idea of a God-given mission to spread its power and influence across the continent, a process Americans referred to as "Manifest Destiny," America coveted what Mexico had. National leaders promoted expansion with an almost religious zeal and developed plans for it. Throughout the 1830s and 1840s, successive presidential administrations and their spokesmen in the press agitated for an America that spanned the continent. All of them presumed that any dispute over land acquired in the process would be settled under the conditions of the Missouri Compromise, namely by the Compromise Line. President John Tyler labored tirelessly for the annexation of Texas under this assumption. Newly independent from Mexico in 1836, Texas waited almost ten years for its repeated petitions to gain a sufficient number of sympathetic ears in Washington. Tyler listened intently and, as the final act of his tenure as president, pushed through Congress a joint resolution for Texas annexation in the spring of 1845. By December of

James Polk was elected president in 1844 on a platform of expansion, and he succeeded in adding the Oregon Territory and California to the United States. The newly acquired territory brought back the issue of whether new states would allow slavery, leading to disagreement, anger, and violence.

that year, Texas gained statehood. Being below the 36°30' line and heavily populated with Southerners, it entered the Union as a slave state.

Tyler's successor, James K. Polk, made expansion the centerpiece of his presidency. Polk ran for office in 1844 on the slogan

"54°40' or Fight," a reference to the proposed border between the United States and British Canada, and a promise to grab the West from Mexico. Once elected, Polk fulfilled both pledges to the greatest extent he could. In 1846, his administration signed a treaty with Great Britain, giving the Oregon Territory, below the 42° line, to the United States. That same year, Polk took the country to war with Mexico. Using a series of transparently provocative and deceptive devices, Polk engineered a war that was understood, even at the time, to be a flagrant land grab. Polk and Manifest Destiny enthusiasts of his type wanted the West; they wanted California.

Signs of trouble appeared within weeks of the opening of hostilities. Polk grasped for a massive tract of land that, much as with the Louisiana Purchase over 40 years earlier, would have to be divided between the North and South. Without a doubt, states would eventually be formed in the West; whether they would be free or slave was the issue. A congressman from Pennsylvania, of all places, stepped forward to propose an organizational model. Having some experience with lines of division between North and South, Pennsylvania's David Wilmot suggested a plan, known as the Wilmot Proviso, which turned on the exclusion of slavery from any and all territory taken from Mexico. As Wilmot might have anticipated, his Proviso elicited a blistering response from his Southern colleagues. The total exclusion of slavery, they fumed, would imprison and impoverish the South by preventing its expansion into an area where cotton might be grown. They accused Wilmot and the North of initiating a program for the slow strangulation of the South's economy and the elimination of slavery. Worse yet, the Proviso seemed to repudiate not only the Missouri Compromise but also the entire concept of using imaginary lines to separate and insulate the competing sections. The Mason-Dixon and Missouri Compromise lines had acted as buffers between colliding realities. The implications of challenging the integrity of those lines were dire. Wilmot's Proviso was rejected in Congress, but it signaled the impending collapse of the conversation between North and South, and pointed out the inherent weakness of a national dialogue based on illusion. Lines on maps and borders drawn in people's minds began to appear insufficient to avoid conflict and, ultimately violence.

The United States won its war with Mexico handily and took control of California officially in 1848; the evaporating significance of imaginary borders and lines of compromise became apparent two years later. California stepped onto the national stage in January 1849, when President Polk announced to the country that gold had been discovered in the foothills of the Sierra Nevada mountains. Polk had barely finished speaking before the greatest internal mass migration in American history began. Within a year, California had a population sufficient to allow for statehood. At that moment, the argument over *when* California would be admitted came to an end, and a far more bitter one, over *how,* began. With its vast gold fields, bustling port of San Francisco, and fertile inland valley, California represented either the perfect Northern or the perfect Southern state. Commerce and industry would flourish in northern California; agriculture had a bright future in the great San Joaquin Valley that stretched into the southern part of the territory. The new state was well suited for either Northern business or Southern cotton growing. Which way California might go was the burning question of the day.

According to the prevailing model of compromise and division, the line that began as the Mason-Dixon and transmuted into the Missouri Compromise Line at the Ohio River should have been simply extended to the shores of the Pacific. The same line that separated North and South from the Chesapeake to the Mississippi should have sliced California into two equal parts, half slave and half free. The problem lay in the fact that southern California, as yet sparsely populated and lacking in resources, had no real potential for immediate growth if detached from the northern gold mines and San Francisco. The slave part of the state would thus be at a serious disadvantage for the foreseeable future, whereas the free portion would thrive from the very beginning. Clear-thinking observers at the time accepted that California had to enter the Union as a single entity. Neither the North nor the South wanted the other section to win that prize. Stalemate and impasse once more resulted.

Sensing the need for his particular brand of political juggling, Henry Clay stepped in. Devoted to the principle of compromise but now less wedded to the idea of lines than he was in 1820, Clay proposed in January 1850 that California be admitted whole as a free state. In return for this boon to the Northern economy, the South won the passage of a strict Fugitive Slave Law that allowed slave holders to reclaim escaped slaves who had crossed into free states. The law furthermore gave owners or their agents the power to compel local officials to help them in their task, even if those authorities refused to help out of moral conviction. Although some people on both sides grumbled about being shortchanged in the deal, Clay's compromise passed and California entered the Union as a free state. Both North and South claimed victory, and Clay congratulated himself on a job well done. Yet in his disregard for compromise lines, first in not partitioning California and then in allowing slave catchers to cross into and operate with impunity in free territory, Clay invalidated almost 100 years of compromise through balance and division. Not extending the Mason-Dixon and Missouri Compromise lines meant that admittedly arbitrary sectional boundaries were no longer untouchable. By ignoring precedent, Clay made any future lines of division subject to trespass and even total erasure in the name of expediency.

The immediate results of the California Compromise, also called the Compromise of 1850, did not bode well for the future. Northerners reacted with angry disbelief to the news that slaveholders and their henchmen now had the authority to enter free territory and force the local population to aid them in recovering escaped slaves. Whether they liked it or not, men and women who found slavery abominable became party to its continued operation; they became unwilling accomplices in what they understood to be an immoral practice. Southerners viewed the

The debate over slavery only intensified throughout the nineteenth century. Southerners fiercely defended their right to hold slaves, while Northern abolitionists worked on freeing slaves through organizations like the Underground Railroad. The "freedom stairway" shown here in Ohio led runaway slaves from the Ohio River to the John Rankin House, one of the stops on the Railroad.

acquisition of California by the free-state bloc as tantamount to theft and as part of a larger Northern conspiracy to control the nation's economy, making it inhospitable to slavery. Many in the South feared that the complete abolition of slavery by preventing its expansion in the West was the ultimate goal of their fellow Americans in the North. Suspicion and resentment soon boiled over into violence.

Three thousand miles from California, the new willingness of Americans to replace compromise lines with gunfire manifested itself in the little Pennsylvania town of Christiana, arguably the place where the first shots of the Civil War were fired. The gun battle that occurred there pitted representatives of two antagonistic worldviews against one another along the oldest dividing line in America. On September 11, 1851, a Maryland slave owner, invoking the Fugitive Slave Law, crossed the Mason-Dixon Line and entered Pennsylvania to retrieve a group of escaped slaves he claimed belonged to him. Convinced that the Marylander's cause was an insult to morality, justice, and everything Pennsylvania stood for, Christiana's free black community joined with white townsfolk to defend the targets of the recovery effort. The parties met one another in broad daylight, fully armed and reconciled to bloodshed. After a fierce fight, in which the Maryland owner was killed, the slave catchers retreated across the Mason-Dixon Line, carrying with them a tale of armed blacks and white Northern disregard for a federal law. Many in the North applauded the resolve of the town's residents in the defense of liberty; Southerners condemned it. Significantly, for the first time, organized violence had been used in the context of the slavery debate.

For decades, the Mason-Dixon Line had meant freedom to black slaves. Crossing it while escaping to the North on the famous Underground Railroad very nearly guaranteed freedom. A life of liberty and hope waited on one side of the line for those leaving behind the numbed existence and degradation of slavery on the other. The Mason-Dixon Line was a border, pure and simple, between freedom and bondage, and no compromise designed to settle a dispute on the other side of the continent was going to change that. What began in California was destined to be settled along this venerable line. The Christiana fight underscored the role of the Mason-Dixon Line in antebellum

America and its symbolic value as a border. Many Americans agreed that the battle in Christiana signaled a much larger and deadlier confrontation yet to come. As one newspaper exclaimed, it was "CIVIL WAR, THE FIRST BLOW STRUCK."[57]

The contest over California and the bloody encounter at Christiana called into question the whole notion of lines effecting compromises in American culture and politics. By the early 1850s, people had begun to lose faith in the type of imaginary boundaries of which the Mason-Dixon served as something of an archetype. California had no use for such devices; the Fugitive Slave Law rendered them impotent. Harder blows came as the organization of the West continued.

Kansas and Nebraska territories offered thousands of square miles of rich farmland and opportunities for success the likes of which America had not seen in decades. What the region did not possess was a clear blueprint for its administration. The primary reason for this was the matter of who would work the land that farmers would soon claim. The slavery issue dogged Kansas and Nebraska, as it had California. The easiest solution to the territories' status would be to honor the Missouri Compromise and extend its line, thus making both places free. The problem was that slave holders in Missouri had an eye on the fields in Kansas. Prohibiting slavery in the territory excluded Missourians from taking advantage of inexpensive acreage just waiting to be tilled. Missouri slave owners, therefore, pressured their representatives in Washington to ignore the compromise that created their state and to pry open Kansas to slavery. Understandably, Northerners opposed any such challenge to the sanctity of the $36°30'$ line, especially after the messy California business. Once again, North and South found themselves at loggerheads over the extension of slavery.

A solution presented itself in the form of a bill submitted to Congress by Senator Stephen Douglas of Illinois. Douglas's motivation lay in his desire to organize the West preparatory to the building of a transcontinental railroad from his home state to California, a project that would pay handsome dividends to

Douglas and to Illinois. When it came to slavery, Douglas was of the mind to let it exist where people wanted it and exclude it where they did not. His plan reflected the senator's essential indifference to slavery's moral implications and a disastrous misreading of the emotions surrounding the issue.

In 1854, Douglas offered his vision to Congress as the Kansas-Nebraska Act. In it, Douglas enshrined a concept he

## TWO STATES LOYAL TO THE UNION

Although thoroughly Southern and to a large extent sympathetic to the Confederate cause, Maryland and its neighbor, Delaware, remained loyal during the Civil War, partly because of the decline of slavery within their borders. Like that of rest of the old Chesapeake, Maryland's economy had gradually moved away from its concentration on cash crops during the course of the nineteenth century. Tobacco, though profitable, was very hard on the soil, draining it of nutrients and slowly reducing the acreage available for planting. Corn and various cereals had become more important parts of the agricultural economy by 1860. As large-scale tobacco cultivation waned, so did Maryland's need for slave labor. Between the American Revolution and the Civil War, the number of free blacks in Maryland rose and the number of slaves declined. The entire region around Maryland, Delaware, and Virginia, in fact, became something of an export market for slaves headed to the cotton plantations of the Deep South, where gang labor was a necessity and in very short supply. This development caused a precipitous decline in the number of slave owners in Maryland. Fewer than 20 percent of the state's households held slaves by 1850. Eleven years later, nearly 50 percent of its black population was free.* Delaware was probably the least Southern border state. Traditionally an appendage of Pennsylvania, Delaware shared little in common with its Confederate cousins. Slavery was almost nonexistent in the state by the Civil War; only 5 percent of Delaware's blacks lived in bondage. Although approximately 1,000 Delaware men volunteered for service in the Confederate cause, more than 10,000 white and 1,000 black Delaware men did likewise for the Union.** Economics kept a vital part of the nation loyal just when loyalty was needed the most.

*Bruce Levine, *Half Slave, Half Free: The Roots of the Civil War* (New York: Hill and Wang, 1992), 39.

**James M. McPherson, *Ordeal by Fire: The Civil War* (New York: Alfred A. Knopf, 1982), 152–153.

called "popular sovereignty": Voters in the territories could decide for themselves whether or not to prohibit slavery without reference to the Missouri Compromise. Imaginary lines need not trouble them. As a Douglas supporter said, the act undercut the whole idea of compromise lines by making the 36°30' division "inoperative and void."[58] The nation had outgrown such mechanisms and the peaceful coexistence they promised. In March, Douglas's bill passed both the House and Senate. The firewall that had insulated each section from the wrath of the other and that had separated slavery and freedom crumbled. Kansas paid the price two years later when vicious clashes between proslavery and antislavery forces gave the territory an unwelcome nickname—Bleeding Kansas.

The Supreme Court's decision in the case of Dred Scott completed the demise of invisible borders as tools for compromise. During its 1857 session, the Court agreed to decide the case involving Scott, a slave who demanded to be freed. At one point in his life, Scott had accompanied his master into a free state, then returned to the South with him. Upon his master's death, Scott sued for his freedom based on his Northern visit; he contended that entering a free state conferred that status on him. In March 1858, the Court officially disagreed. Writing for the majority, Chief Justice Roger B. Taney not only rejected Scott's claim but went one step further to reject Congress's power to prohibit slavery anywhere in the United States. Taney declared that, irrespective of the Missouri Compromise or any other such political fiction, slave owners had the right to travel where they desired without fear of relinquishing their "property." At one stroke, the Supreme Court decimated 38 years of compromise and struck down an article of faith, namely, that North and South could hide from each other behind and within contrived borders. With this decision, the Court erased every such line America had ever drawn and every boundary that had ever given them hope for an ultimate compromise between the sections. Nothing now stood between the two divergent, hostile ways of life. Lines created by surveyors and politicians had first blurred, then faded, and now disappeared. To be sure, new ones would be penned in their place, but these would be battle lines laid out by generals.

**8**

# The Mason-Dixon
# Line at War

The crises of the 1850s effectively erased the lines that Americans had been drawing in their vain attempt to avoid a clash over slavery. The fantasy of compromise evaporated at the same time. How much this all mattered by 1860 is unclear; most people had already given up on compromise. Compromise seemed strangely antiquated, like the lines that had exemplified its central concepts of balance and division. Stephen Douglas certainly did not miss it. Douglas viewed his wiping away of the Mason-Dixon and Missouri Compromise lines as a positive stride toward the future. During his 1858 reelection campaign, Douglas exhorted Americans to

> blot out these lines of North and South, and resort back to these lines of State boundaries which the Constitution marked out, and engraved upon the face of the country; have no other dividing lines than these, and we will be one united, harmonious people ...59

Douglas acted on his assumptions in the Kansas-Nebraska Act, but his underlying faith in the possibility of avoiding a violent contest between the sections was ill advised. Lines of demarcation and division existed for good reason up to the Civil War. They served as a concrete expression of what Americans already implicitly understood: The republic had essentially evolved into two hostile lands that required some type of mutually recognized barrier between them. Absent that, they were headed toward war.

Oddly, the political demise of the concept of lines heightened its popular allure. As history forced North and South together, former lines of compromise reemerged as quasi-national borders, with all the emotional energy such a change entailed. The growing sense that a collision loomed between the sections, one that would profoundly alter the political, social, and cultural landscape of America, amplified this newfound significance. Future Secretary of State William Seward, a New York senator at the time, gave voice to this still somewhat vague sensation of impending change and almost certain violence at the

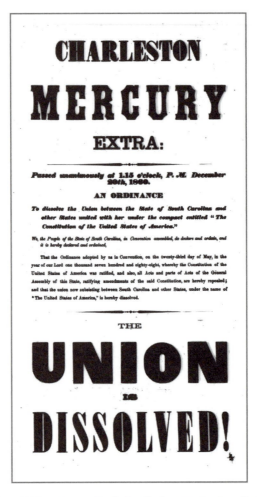

This flier from 1860 announces South Carolina's secession from the Union which led to the creation of the Confederate States of America. South Carolina initiated the Civil War between the Union and the Confederacy on April 12, 1861, when it attacked the federal garrison at Fort Sumter.

same time that Douglas was lauding a lineless map of the United States. Seward described America in 1858 as

> a theater which exhibits in full operation two radically differ-
> ent political systems: the one resting on the basis of servile
> labor, the other on the basis of voluntary labor of free men ...

these antagonistic systems are continually coming into close
contact, and collision results.[60]

Seward knew that what he called "an irrepressible conflict"
would take place along the very lines Douglas disparaged. In
fact, the upcoming war would, in a sense, reinvigorate them by
exaggerating their symbolic value—none more so than the venerable Mason-Dixon Line.

The American union began disintegrating one month after
Abraham Lincoln became the president-elect. In December
1860, South Carolina made good on its threat to secede if an
antislavery candidate ever won the presidency. Declaring itself to
be "a separate and independent state," South Carolina set itself
up as a rallying point for a Southern confederacy. Other
Southern states, in perfect agreement with South Carolina's
announced goal of preserving slavery, followed the Palmetto
State out of the Union: Georgia, Alabama, Louisiana, Florida,
and Mississippi seceded in January 1861; Texas left a month
later. On February 8, the seceding states met in convention in
Montgomery, Alabama, and declared themselves the
Confederate States of America. The Confederacy selected
Jefferson Davis as its first, last, and only president.

Though ruptured and battered, a vestige of the old border
between North and South still held. Along the Mason-Dixon
and Missouri Compromise lines, slave states hesitated.
Americans living along the line acknowledged that the sectional
differences that had carried the nation to this point were irre-
versible, but secession meant civil war, and that was another
matter entirely. The border states, as they were known, recoiled
from the idea of dissolving the Union. Missouri had begun its
life as the child of compromise actuated by the $36°30'$ line.
However deeply divided in its sympathies and despite its determination to maintain slavery within its bounds, Missouri
refrained from joining its neighbors in secession. Kentucky also
remained loyal. The tier of states immediately below them—
Arkansas, Tennessee, North Carolina, and Virginia—took a

wait-and-see attitude, promising to stay if no attempt were made by the federal government to force the seceding states back into the Union. Unlike the true border areas, these states felt a closer connection to the Confederacy, and their people were less severely split in their allegiance to slavery as an institution.

Like its extension to the west, the Mason-Dixon Line functioned as a border between a loyal slave state and the rest of the Union. Maryland, sandwiched between hotbeds of Union and Confederate sentiment, felt perhaps more conflicted than any other border state. Attached to the federal government by historical and geographic bonds (Washington, D.C., was located within its borders), Maryland nevertheless remained a thoroughly Southern state. Without a doubt, slavery was dying in the state: The percentage of slaves in the total Chesapeake slave population had dropped from 30 percent during the Revolutionary period to a mere 15 percent by 1860, and there were more free blacks there than in Virginia, which had a much higher number of blacks overall.[61] Still, Marylanders embraced the institution of slavery, or more precisely the racial order and class hierarchy it had produced, as tightly as any other Southern state. Even an issue as momentous as the continued integrity of the United States could not wash away 200 years of identity formation. Marylanders thought Northern but felt Southern. Although Maryland's head knew that progress lay in the course charted by the Northern states, its heart seemed drawn inevitably to the South. In many ways, Maryland looked to fellow Southerners to rescue it from its attachment to the North. A popular song during the Civil War, entitled "We'll Be Free in Our Maryland," expressed just how deeply many in Maryland longed to reinforce their Southern ties:

> The boys down South in Dixie's land/Will come and rescue
> Maryland
> We'll drink a toast to one and all/Keep cock'd and prim'd
> for the Southern call
> The day will come, we'll make a stand/Then we'll be
> free in Maryland.[62]

However reluctant to join the Confederacy Maryland may have been, or unsure about secession, it remained a part of the South. Just on the other side of the Mason-Dixon Line lay Pennsylvania. A long history of abolitionism, a reputation as a haven for runaway slaves, and the memories of the Christiana riot made Pennsylvania an exemplary free state. Fiercely devoted to the cause of Union and freedom, the state embodied everything that the South fought against. Industry, commerce, finance, urbanization, and immigration put Pennsylvania squarely in league with the other Northern states and made it stand out in Southern minds as a symbol of Northern dominance. The state also served as the gateway to the North, a natural funnel through which an army invading from the south might pour into the urban core of the country. In real and imagined terms, then, Pennsylvania drew all the wrong kinds of attention from the new Confederacy, attention that would very shortly redraw the Mason-Dixon Line in blood. The fact that Pennsylvania and Maryland were technically allies did not change matters. The two states bristled at one another across the Mason-Dixon Line, agents of two warring cultures, united in name only. When war came, of course, men from both places would answer the Union's call to arms; an equal number of white Marylanders fought for the North as for the South, but that only served to illustrate how slavery and a powerful Southern heritage divided Maryland's loyalties.

At precisely 4:30 A.M. on the morning of April 12, 1861, a gunner touched off a cannon on the shores of Charleston harbor in South Carolina. The ball it fired whistled through the air and detonated against the walls of Fort Sumter, a U.S. Army fortress situated on an island just offshore. The state of South Carolina had attacked a federal garrison; the American Civil War was under way. The bombardment of Fort Sumter pressed a decision on the Southern states that had as yet resisted the call to secede. Now they had to choose whether to stay in the Union or leave. Except for the border states, they left, most important among them Virginia. Along with Tennessee, Arkansas, and North

After seceding from the Union, the Confederacy chose Richmond, Virginia as its capital and selected Jefferson Davis, seen here in an 1860 portrait, as president. Virginia was one of the most important states in the Confederacy, possessing the wealthiest, best-educated men and essential industries, horses, and food.

Carolina, Virginia joined the Confederacy in the spring of 1861. It was the real prize. As the wealthiest, best-educated, and most politically sophisticated Southern state, Virginia was the real prize. Additionally, Virginia possessed vast quantities of the men, industry, horses, and food that the Confederacy so desperately needed. Furthermore, geography gave Virginia pride of place in the overall Southern strategy for victory and independence. Sharing a long border with Maryland and partially surrounding the federal capital, Virginia became central to Confederate war plans. Bearing all this in mind, the Confederate Congress moved the Southern capital from Montgomery to Richmond, putting it within 75 miles of its Union counterpart. The proximity of the capitals, Virginia's natural position as a springboard into Pennsylvania, and the vulnerability of the Mason-Dixon Line that resulted from Maryland's allegiance to the South made certain that the eastern theater was where the Civil War would be decided.

The Virginia border now became that of the Confederacy, but the true border of the South remained between Maryland and Pennsylvania along the Mason-Dixon Line. Both sides needed to control it. Lincoln, for his part, had to hold on to Maryland, regardless of the cost. If Maryland swung over to the rebels, the other slaveholding border states just might follow suit. Such an outcome would cost the federal cause dearly: If Maryland, Kentucky, and Missouri went over to the Confederacy, the rebels stood to gain 45 percent in their white population, 80 percent in factory output, and 40 percent more horses for their already formidable cavalry.[63] Losing Maryland would also endanger Pennsylvania, perhaps even Philadelphia, and would surely result in the evacuation of Washington to avoid its capture. Whatever it took, Maryland had to stay in the Union. The Mason-Dixon Line could not be allowed to become the de facto southern border of the United States.

Lincoln's task would not be easy. Maryland seethed contempt for the federal government, and pro-Confederate sympathies ran high among its citizens. Southern sentiment percolated up throughout the state. No sooner had the war begun than 20,000 Marylanders volunteered to fight for the Confederacy.[64] At home, violence flared. Anti-Union mobs in Baltimore ambushed one of the first regiments to heed Lincoln's call for volunteers in April, 1861, resulting in the deaths of 4 soldiers and 12 civilians. Saboteurs repeatedly burned vital bridges leading into Washington and cut telegraph lines to hamper the federal buildup and disrupt communications. Supporters of the Southern cause in Maryland made their presence known and posed a very real danger to the Union war effort.

No one realized this more fully or swiftly than Lincoln; he moved quickly and boldly to suppress pro-Confederate activity and reassert federal control of Maryland. After the Baltimore riot, the president suspended the writ of habeas corpus in the most troublesome parts of Maryland. Arrests could now be made more easily and suspects held indefinitely without being specifically charged. On May 13, Lincoln declared martial law in Baltimore. The following September, the government arrested 31 Maryland legislators suspected of plotting to aid an impending Confederate invasion of the state. By initiating extreme measures, considered by many at the time and since to be unconstitutional, Lincoln made it clear that he intended to keep Maryland in the Union and the Confederacy away from the Mason-Dixon Line.

In Richmond, the Confederate capital, Maryland figured just as prominently in the blueprint for overall victory. President Jefferson Davis and his generals knew that Maryland had to be taken. Not only would crucial supplies and manpower be gained, but the federal capital would be surrounded and the northeastern seaboard opened to raids in force, if not outright invasion. Striking into Pennsylvania from a Confederate Maryland, a rebel army could seize supplies, ruin federal communications, and sow panic and confusion among the population. Of greater value was the symbolic victory inherent in crossing the Mason-Dixon Line. At a single stroke, so Davis and the Confederate leadership imagined, the rebels might throw the Northern armies on the defensive, puncture Northern morale, and lift the spirits of the Confederate public. Rolling with impunity across the Mason-Dixon Line, the Confederate armies would offer a testament to Southern power and call into question the physical security of the North. In this scenario, the Mason-Dixon Line took on almost magical properties—cross it, and Southern fighting superiority would be demonstrated and the futility of forced reunion confirmed.

Any move to the North, however, posed so many risks that Davis needed to be prodded into taking action. Davis understood the South's inferiority to the North in every major military area. In terms of men and material, the Confederacy fell woefully short. With miles of coastline and no navy to speak of, it was vulnerable to naval blockade as well. Shortages of troops and supplies could be expected, increasing the value of the limited stocks the South had. Davis did not have the luxury of fighting an offensive war of the type needed in Maryland, no matter how attractive the prize; he had to husband his resources carefully. The Confederate president and his generals recognized that the best strategy for the South was a defensive one, in which all they had to do was not lose. Of course, the South could not hold out forever, but a long, bitterly fought war in which Lincoln and his armies had to be on the offensive constantly might compel the federal government to expend more energy and blood than the continued union was worth. If the defensive tack did not produce the desired effect, however, the Confederate commanders were instructed to strike when and where the opportunity presented itself. Thus was born what military historians refer to as the South's offensive-defensive strategy.

The Confederacy's novel approach to fighting the war made an attack across the Mason-Dixon Line eminently logical if the timing and circumstances were right. First, Davis needed the right tool for the job. Robert E. Lee advertised himself and his Army of Northern Virginia as that tool. One of Davis's most trusted commanders, Lee rallied the defenses of Richmond in the spring of 1862 and turned back a major Union effort to capture the capital. He then approached Davis about an invasion of Maryland. A strike there would rouse Confederate sympathizers, threaten Washington, D.C., and distract Lincoln and his generals from other operations and duties. Southern morale and hopes

Guard House & Guard. 107th U.S. Colored I. I. T.

The South had to be very careful with its resources during the war, as the North had more money, more supplies, more factories, and a navy to target miles and miles of Southern coastline. Most importantly, the North had more men, especially after Lincoln issued the Emancipation Proclamation in 1862, prompting black soldiers, like these of the 107th Colored Infantry, to enter the army for the Union.

for victory would soar if Lee punched into Maryland and subsequently across the Mason-Dixon Line into the *real* North: Pennsylvania. The psychological victory inherent in crossing the line might help end the war by pointing out its futility to the Northern public. Lee, in fact, wrote to Davis, saying that a victory in Pennsylvania "would enable the people of the United States to determine ... whether they will support" politicians who favored continuing the war or "those who wish to bring it to a termination."[65] Lincoln saw this clearly. He ordered his generals to chase down Lee and "destroy the rebel army"[66] before it even got close to Pennsylvania.

Moving from his base in Virginia, Lee entered Maryland and headed for the Mason-Dixon Line. Along the way, Lee tried to convince the people of Maryland that he came as a liberator. He issued an address, "To the People of Maryland," in which he assured them that he came to right "the wrongs that have been inflicted upon the citizens of a commonwealth allied to the States of the South by the strongest social, political, and commercial ties...."[67] He made no mention of the strongest tie, slavery. The Union and Confederate armies finally met in battle at the same tiny creek in Maryland that Mason and Dixon had noted in their journal a hundred years before. At Antietam

## LOSING HEARTS AND MINDS

No informed Confederate leader, military or political, believed that an invasion of the North in 1862 via Maryland would be easy. Robert E. Lee, perhaps more than others, knew that any such move would require more than military power and sound, careful planning. Once in Maryland, Lee understood that he would have to win the hearts and sympathies of its people. This promised to be difficult at best, given the fact that the military situation dictated an invasion route through western Maryland, a part of the state rife with pro-Union sentiment. The whole point of attacking there was to swing around the Army of the Potomac's main body concentrated between Washington and Richmond, relieving the pressure on the Confederate capital and compelling Lincoln to fear for the safety of his own. Doing so, however, meant moving through territory that might turn out to be hostile or at best unwelcoming. Lee, therefore, ordered his men to be on their best behavior. Marylanders and their property were to be respected, and a good impression was to be made on the local population. Unfortunately, try though they might, the Confederate troops were received with no slight degree of disdain by the Marylanders along their line of march. Among other things, the disheveled appearance of the soldiers did not sit well with the orderly farmers and townspeople. One of these locals commented with disgust that Lee's army must have been "the filthiest set of men and officers I ever saw ... they smelt all over the [town]."* Another sore point was the relative worthlessness of the Confederate money soldiers used to purchase goods from merchants and farmers. The Army of Northern Virginia's failure to endear itself to the Marylanders has led James McPherson to conclude that the "silent response" that greeted Lee "constituted the first failure of the invasion."** The final one came at Antietam.

James McPherson, *Battle Cry of Freedom: The Civil War Era* (New York: Oxford University Press, 1988), 535–536.

**Ibid., 536.

Creek, on September 17, 1862, George McClellan's Army of the Potomac fought Lee to a standstill in the bloodiest single-day battle in American history. The two forces pummeled each other, leaving the field soaked in blood and covered with bodies, but at the end of it all, McClellan checked Lee's advance and prevented a Confederate invasion of Pennsylvania. For his efforts, Lee lost upward of 13,700 men at Antietam; some of his commanders reported half of their men dead or wounded when the guns fell silent. The next day, Lee began a cautious retreat into Virginia while a regimental band played "Maryland, My Maryland."[68]

Stung by defeat, Lee remained fixated on the notion of crossing the Mason-Dixon Line and invading the North. His staff members, Southern politicians, and the Confederate public agreed. The Mason-Dixon Line retained its deadly allure; striking into Pennsylvania persisted as a psychological and strategic goal of the first order. On the other side of the line, defending Pennsylvania and keeping Maryland in the Union remained key elements in the federal government's strategic thinking. Pennsylvania had to be shored up as a bulwark against invasion; Maryland had to be preserved as a part of the South that was loyal to the Union. The government had to keep the Mason-Dixon Line secure as an imaginary border between two parts of the same country. Anything else would confer legitimacy on the South and probably convince Northerners that the war could not be won.

Lee and the Confederacy felt confident enough to make a second try at invasion in the summer of 1863. Encouraged by victories at Fredericksburg and Chancellorsville, and buoyed by the dogged resistance offered by the Mississippi port city of Vicksburg to a powerful Union siege, Lee took the Army of Northern Virginia into Maryland once again, and from there into Pennsylvania. His overall plan called for extended raiding, disruption of Union supply and communication lines, and in general just causing as much havoc as possible. He also hoped at some point for a decisive battle that would prove to the

Northern public that the Confederacy could not be brought to heel through force of arms. Lee's goal was to gain simultaneous psychological and military victories by punching through the Mason-Dixon Line and rampaging for a while in Pennsylvania. Well thought out though it was, the plan disintegrated near a small town that did not even exist when Mason and Dixon passed through the area. It was called Gettysburg.

The battle of Gettysburg began as an accidental encounter between elements of Lee's army and the Army of the Potomac, now commanded by George Meade. It developed into a vicious and bloody three-day engagement in which Lee squandered an early advantage and suffered the consequences. Days one and two of the battle (July 1 and 2, 1863) saw Lee roll the Union army into a defensive "fishhook" just south of Gettysburg. Nearly encircled and desperately defending his flanks against furious assaults, Meade held his ground. On day three, a frustrated Lee launched a courageous but futile attack against the center of the Union line. On July 3, he ordered General George Pickett to lead a frontal assault uphill at a place called Cemetery Ridge, directly into the cannons and massed muskets of Meade's main body. When the day was over, two-thirds of Pickett's men lay dead on the field. The Union controlled Gettysburg, and Lee was forced to acknowledge defeat. He later apologized to his battered army, mournfully exclaiming "It's all my fault."[69] Mauled and despondent, Lee gave up the dream of invading the North and fell back into Virginia. Almost 30,000 of Lee's men did not return with him. As his army dragged itself home, news came that Vicksburg had fallen, the Confederacy had been cut in two, and a Union army under Ulysses S. Grant, the man to whom Lee would surrender in April 1865, was advancing into the heart of the Confederacy. The fate of the rebellion was sealed.

Crossed and crossed again, punctured and repaired, the Mason-Dixon Line remained intact during the Civil War. Indeed, it had, in a certain sense, arisen from the ashes of the crises of the 1850s to once more stand as a crucial, if imaginary, border. The Confederacy's defeat, however, brought a new wrinkle to the role of the Mason-Dixon Line role. From 1865 on, the Mason-Dixon Line took shape in people's minds as a boundary between a victorious, now-ascendant North and a defeated, subjugated South. The prewar image of the line as a border between equals was replaced by a new concept in which the South assumed the role of victim. History had betrayed the South, so the defeated Confederates believed. The North had won technically, they argued, but the South had not been won over. "Dixie," as the South came to call itself, would rise again not to defend a way of life but to lament a Lost Cause.

# 9

# "Dixie" and
# the Lost Cause

Almost 80 years after the end of the Civil War, Bernadine Flanagan, a young black woman from New London, Connecticut, was riding on a train through Pennsylvania. Like thousands of other patriotic American women, Flanagan had joined the Women's Army Corps (WAC) during World War II. The train she rode that day was carrying her and other women volunteers, white and black, to a training camp below the Mason-Dixon Line. As they neared the Maryland border, the women experienced the uneasy sensation of approaching an internal border, a frontier of sorts between two realities. Flanagan remembered how, as the train rolled south, its passengers "were separated when we got to the Mason-Dixon Line. I was told I had to move to another section of the train...."[70] At that moment, the young servicewoman knew that she was leaving the North and entering the South. Flanagan and the other women were crossing a line that had been erased in crisis, bloodied in war, and resurrected in peace. In many ways, the Mason-Dixon Line she crossed that day possessed more symbolic power than ever before. The geographical fiction it defined harbored more mythical qualities; no longer just the South, it was now Dixie. Dixie embodied an idealized past, a comforting illusion that sheltered Southerners from the change sweeping through their land. The Mason-Dixon Line reflected and circumscribed a reactionary Southern identity bent on resisting the pull of modernity and served as a convenient marker for the boundary between reality and an imagined past.

The rebuilding of Richmond had scarcely begun before Southerners began reconstituting collective and individual identities every bit as shattered as their cities and as devastated as their farms. Much more had been destroyed than the political entity known as the Confederacy. An idea of what it meant to be Southern had perished as well. Out of the rubble of war, Southerners had to craft a new self-image, one that offered comfort in troubling times and pride in the midst of humiliation. They had to develop a revised vocabulary that would enable them to give voice to a collective sense of self and purpose. New

Years after the end of the Civil War and the emancipation of slaves, the Mason-Dixon Line retained meaning as a cultural and racial boundary line. This 1939 photograph shows an African-American man forced to use a special entrance to a Mississippi movie theater because of his race.

assumptions, beliefs, and ideas were needed to stabilize and direct a society cut adrift from everything that had provided it with meaning. A revived Mason-Dixon Line figured prominently in the ideological and emotional reconstruction of the South—and in the myth of the Lost Cause.

The postwar South groped for guiding principles and fresh sociocultural reference points that would allow it to transcend defeat. Wrenched from tradition and thrust reluctantly onto the path of modernity, Southerners in the late nineteenth and early twentieth centuries reacted in two ways. On the one hand were men and women who recognized that the old South had disappeared forever. These people welcomed the blank slate created by the destruction of the antebellum way of life. They looked north and thought they saw a comprehensive social model that, if carefully applied, might bring stability, security, and prosperity to the states of the now-defunct Confederacy. Supporters of this point of view christened it the New South movement. New South proponents envisaged a refashioned Southern landscape of cities, factories, and commerce that was fully integrated into a bustling national economy. They admired Northern energy and initiative and hoped that their native South might emulate Northern qualities. One New South promoter remembered how a brief prewar visit above the Mason-Dixon Line to Pennsylvania had made the envy boil up inside him. Looking around, he recalled longing for the day when Southerners "would cultivate their farms more and better, and educate their sons and daughters, like the people of [Pennsylvania]."[71] New South enthusiasts wanted to move beyond divisive borders such as the Mason-Dixon Line and remake the South in the North's image.

However optimistic and sensible their message, New South supporters remained in the minority. Most of them had admired the North since before the war, and they had never really absorbed the culture and values of their ancestors. Their forward-facing, buoyant confidence appealed to Southerners far less than the honeyed nostalgia and comforting self-deception of the Lost Cause. An amalgam of heroic images, repackaged hopes, and half-truths, the Lost Cause encapsulated a message of Southern grandeur and exceptionalism. Within the myth's story line, the South emerged as an almost sacrificial victim prostrate on the altar of Northern greed. The Lost Cause spoke to a persistent Southern belief that, although raw military and industrial power resided in the North, honor, dignity, and righteousness were rooted in Southern soil. The old South's cause, though lost, had been just and good. With its emphasis on Southern chauvinism and retrenchment, the myth set itself in stark opposition to the central tenets of the New South ideology. The Lost Cause, in effect, reconfigured the antebellum relationship between North and South. In the process, it reinvigorated and gave renewed meaning to the Mason-Dixon Line.

To say that the Civil War had destroyed the South would be an understatement. The Southern order that had evolved over a

200-year period had been literally swept away, its political order made inoperative, its social structure eroded, and its cultural foundation leveled. After 1867, the states that made up the Confederacy were occupied by heavily armed federal troops who enforced the law on the point of a bayonet. The newly freed and empowered black underclass reminded white Southerners of their gutted economy and collapsed slavery-based culture at every turn. The postwar influx of Northern capitalists, referred to disparagingly as "carpetbaggers," gave the region the aura of a conquered territory. The South was frustrated and confused.

Deluged by change, the South found solace in the romantic cult of victimization implicit in the Lost Cause. "Myths," writes Gary Gallagher, "arise when people draw on images and symbols to construct a usable truth, which in turn permits them to deal with traumatic events such as the Confederacy's defeat."[72] So it was with the Lost Cause. Its peculiar mythology consoled Southerners: Slavery had not precipitated the war, and slaves had been happy in their degradation; the Confederate soldiers had fought for liberty against overwhelming odds, and that is the reason they lost; justice and morality had fallen victim to Northern corruption. Within this delusional framework, the Mason-Dixon Line reemerged as an ideological-cultural boundary. As such, the line marked out neither a section nor an imagined nation but rather a fictional place called Dixie, a fantasy world located primarily in the words of a song.

Although the origins of the term *Dixie* are uncertain, its attachment to a specific place and its reflection of a peculiar identity are not. Dixie might or might not refer directly to the Mason-Dixon Line, but there can be no doubt that the line represented the precise geographic border of the South described in the song by the same name. True, the tune's writer, Daniel Decatur Emmet, was not even from the South (he hailed from Ohio), but the words he put on paper described what Southerners imagined their home and themselves to be. According to at least one music expert, the "first verse [of "Dixie"] made it a Southern anthem,"[73] certainly, but it became an anthem only for those Southerners who clung to the Lost Cause myth. As yet another commentator has concluded, "music is not independent of its culture." When it came to the song "Dixie," "white people took it and used it to mean something."[74]

The something "Dixie" meant was an imaginary South insulated against change. Emmet's song expressed a longing to be "away down south in Dixie," the "land of cotton." As the songwriter said, "old times there are not forgotten." It was a place, finally, to "live and die" for. The problem with all this is that the place yearned for and the way of life advertised never existed; rather, both lived only in the minds of Lost Cause advocates. It is significant that "Dixie," written by Emmet in 1859, never caught on in the antebellum South and only became popular after the war forced Southerners to construct a new emotional framework. It became the South's anthem after the guns had fallen silent. The words contain the essence of an unformed Southern identity just beginning to coalesce in the immediate postwar period. According to Lloyd A. Hunter, only after total defeat in 1865 did "Dixie," along with the Confederate battle flag and Confederate gray, become "religious emblems, symbolic of the holy cause and of sacrifices made on its behalf."[75] Thus, "Dixie" became central to Lost Cause mythology, signaling a return to the sectional imagery in which the Mason-Dixon Line identified the South as unique. One did indeed have to go way down South to reach Dixie and cross the Mason-Dixon Line in the process.

Dixie became a refuge of sorts in the Southern imagination, home to honorable folk whose lineage proved their personal and collective worth. Many Southerners, in fact, came to view themselves and their ancestors as something of an Anglo-Saxon elite. Edward A. Pollard, the first in a long line of Southern apologists, popularized the Lost Cause as a contest between a South superior in virtue and breeding and a decadent, ethnically inferior North. In *The Lost Cause: A New Southern History of the War of the Confederates* (1866), Pollard argued that American history recognized an inherent antipathy between the descendents of swashbuckling Cavaliers in the South and greedy Puritan shop-keepers in the North. Much separated these antagonists, "the division being coincident with the line that separated the slave-holding from the non-slave-holding states." What was essentially the Mason-Dixon Line was viewed as separating "two nations of opposite civilizations ... two very different peoples...." To the north resided the descendents of money-grubbing, tight-lipped Puritans, "coarse and materialistic." South of the line lay a "noble

## KLAN TERROR

A vicious and lethal outgrowth of the Lost Cause myth took form as the Ku Klux Klan. Founded in 1866 in Pulaski, Tennessee, and led by the former Confederate general Nathan Bedford Forrest, the Klan dedicated itself to "defending" the South against a future of racial and social progress. Drawing on the Lost Cause contention that the pure and just South had fallen prey to Northern ruthlessness and greed, the Ku Klux Klan proposed to turn back time and reverse the outcome of the war. Between 1866 and 1871, its hooded thugs rampaged through the South, burning, beating, whipping, and murdering anyone who challenged the racial and class structures left over from the old Confederacy. People at the time noted how the Klan became "a nameless terror among negroes [and] poor whites."* The Klansmen, for their part, justified their orgy of bloodshed and intimidation by painting themselves as moral avengers, compelled by injustice to lash out at their enemies. "It is, indeed, unfortunate," the Klan's supporters claimed, that the group's bullies and assassins had "to have recourse to measures of violence and blood to do away with lawless tyrants." "But who is to blame?" so they asked rhetorically. "Assuredly not we people of the South, who have suffered wrongs beyond endurance. Radicalism and negroism ... are alone to blame ... These northern emissaries of advanced political ideas, and of progressive social reforms ... have met the fate they deserved."** Today, descendents of these original American terrorists still fly the Confederate battle flag and still long for the Dixie that never was.

*Eric Foner, *Reconstruction: America's Unfinished Revolution, 1863–1877* (New York: Harper andRow, 1988), 342.

**James M. McPherson, *Ordeal by Fire: Reconstruction* (New York: Alfred A. Knopf, 1982), 544.

type of civilization," made possible by slavery, in which elegant, genteel Southerners exhibited "higher sentimentalism and ... superior refinements of scholarship and manners" than their Northern contemporaries. Pollard's line divided tradition from a "superficial and restless" modernity, thus conferring upon the South "the mark of the superior civilization."[76] So it was that the Mason-Dixon Line evolved from a mere map line into a wall between Northern "degeneracy" and Southern "grace."

Dixie identified a place; the Lost Cause provided that place with a functional mythology. The Mason-Dixon Line catalyzed the mythologizing process by serving as a point beyond which one entered the world of either the Northern or Southern "other." This reference point, of course, had no real meaning other than its marking of the Pennsylvania-Maryland border, but even as such, it outlined distinct worldviews. Maryland, it is true, counted itself among the first Southern states to be reorganized politically after the war, but it nonetheless followed the rest of the South in repudiation of the spirit and goals of Reconstruction, chief among these being racial equality under the law. As early as 1867, Maryland maneuvered itself into a position where it could deprive its black citizens of their rights. Marylanders elected to power white supremacists in the Democratic Party, denied equal educational opportunities to black children, and in the 1867 state constitution redrew its legislative map to give an advantage to white landowners of the old plantation era. As one disgruntled Marylander phrased it, "This is progress backwards...."[77] In contrast, just across the Mason-Dixon Line, Pennsylvania pushed forward on guaranteeing civil rights and social equality to black Americans. Despite having to overcome the same racial obstacles as the rest of the North, Pennsylvania led the way in desegregating its public accommodations in 1867 when it prohibited segregation on public streetcars. Maryland never took even this first, unsteady step toward racial justice—hence Bernadine Flanagan's forced transfer to a blacks-only railway car when she reached the Mason-Dixon Line on her journey South, ironically to offer her services in defense of liberty.

After Lee's surrender at Appomattox in 1865, the Mason-Dixon Line should have been drained of its power and legitimacy as a boundary. Technically, the Union was whole and without sectional division. If the proponents of the New South had gained control over the development that took place during the postwar years, the Mason-Dixon Line certainly would have slipped into historical insignificance and obscurity by the early twentieth century. The myth of the Lost Cause, however, breathed new life into the old line and allowed the compound word "Mason-Dixon" to reenter the Southern lexicon as a cultural point of reference for a mythical place called Dixie.

# 10

# Binding the Wound

## The Mason-Dixon Line Today

Abraham Lincoln's brief address at Gettysburg, according to Garry Wills, should be read as a "stunning verbal coup."[78] Doubtless, the speech given that November day by an exhausted and troubled president contained "words that remade America," as the title of Wills's book claims. The transformation he alludes to, however, went far beyond revised definitions of what it meant to be an American, and began not on the occasion of a cemetery dedication but during a celebratory speech marking electoral victory. One year after his visit to Pennsylvania, Lincoln ran for and won reelection. In his inaugural address, the president exhorted his countrymen to put away the sectional animosities that had cost the country so much blood. Lincoln challenged his listeners to build a new American ideal based on commonality rather than difference. He set before his audience the task of reconstructing the battered republic "with malice toward none" and implored them to "strive on to finish the work we are in, to bind up the nation's wounds."[79]

The arduous process of making the United States whole again entailed the obliteration, both as a concept and as a functioning social device, of dividing lines exemplified by the Mason-Dixon Line. The Mason-Dixon Line epitomized antagonism, suspicion, and separation. It began as a mere colonial border but came to symbolize the divergent social, cultural, and economic paths taken by developing America. The line represented a bargaining chip in the ultimately unsuccessful quest for compromise between freedom and slavery, and it was erased by the crisis that ensued. Its legacy took center stage during the Civil War. Later it fed a myth created to cushion the blows of that war's aftermath in the South. The Mason-Dixon Line indeed had a long and tumultuous existence punctuated by discord and violence. Today, however, the Mason-Dixon Line is fading into insignificance, its existence noted in the pages of high school textbooks and seen in a string of barely legible stone markers, tilting this way and that in out-of-the-way places along the border between Pennsylvania and Maryland. The Mason-Dixon Line, like all artifacts of human society and culture, is dissolving in the acid bath of history.

The changes that came over American society in the wake of World War II hastened the demise of the Mason-Dixon Line. The civil rights movement of the 1950s and 1960s forced Northerners and Southerners alike to confront the legacy of slavery. Men such as Martin Luther King, Jr., helped shatter the Lost Cause myth by taking the country across the Mason-Dixon Line to see firsthand the corrupt, repressive, and backward world the line defined and epitomized. The Old South and its racist institutions could hide no more. Television and other forms of modern communication neither recognized nor respected imaginary lines. The prying eye of the television camera could not be kept from penetrating the darkest recesses of Southern society and culture. Across the land, Americans watched as the anger and hate implicit in the Lost Cause poured out onto the heads of civil rights advocates. They saw fire hoses and dogs turned loose on innocent people; they witnessed beatings and burnings. In this sense, technology transcended the Mason-Dixon Line in ways previously impossible. It continues to do so today.

Modern America affords little space to quaint relics of the past, such as the Mason-Dixon Line. The world it helped delineate and define is gone. North and South no longer exist as polar extremes of social and cultural development. Time itself has created a new American context, a web of relationships that has rendered the very idea of a separate North and South meaningless, but it has done so through a blend of communication technology and economics; this particular blend has generated centripetal forces that are pulling people and places together rather than pushing them apart. Similarity and homogeneity are rapidly supplanting the differences that once nurtured powerful symbolic boundaries like the Mason-Dixon Line. All borders are being challenged in the twenty-first century, whether spatial or psychological, on paper or in people's imaginations. Dividing lines everywhere today are crossed with increasing ease and impunity. Arbitrary lines drawn hundreds of years ago by extinct political entities, such as the Mason-Dixon Line, are the most endangered of them all.

Today, the separation between the North and South is disappearing due in large part to technology and economic globalization. The Mason-Dixon Line is no longer an emotionally and politically charged boundary but now just the border between Pennsylvania and Maryland. This stone with the Maryland emblem is one of the original markers that established the Mason-Dixon Line.

The contrasts between North and South, once so stark, are evaporating with incredible speed, hastened along not only by structural changes in communications and economics but also by demographic trends that are pulling people together into shared environments. Telephones, once a novelty, are found in almost every home in the country (94 percent of homes have telephone service), making possible a degree of instantaneous long-distance communication unique in history. People can talk to practically anyone, anywhere, at any time of their choosing. Television (found in 99 percent of the country's homes) is arguably the most pervasive single medium ever created. It not only connects people, as telephones do, but also essentially neutralizes regional differences in language and culture, offering in the place of diversity a unitary set of symbols, ideals, and expectations. The televised world is one in which people, regardless of geography, participate in a communal experience within a single interpretative framework. Whether one lives in Alabama or New York, Maryland or Pennsylvania, the show is always the same, and so are the values and beliefs embedded within it. Television standardizes life and fosters a sort of leveling. In short, television provides a coherent worldview and cultural vocabulary to anyone with a set in his or her living room, no matter where that living room might be.

Similarly, cyberspace functions as an arena where differences associated with geography are muted. The Internet advertises itself as the medium through which ideas and insights flow unimpeded down a virtual highway that is constricted neither by time nor space. Borders, boundaries, even time zones mean nothing when one "logs on." Being, in effect, a global forum, the Internet undermines belief systems and ideologies dependent on cultural isolation and tradition. Closed, insular precincts cannot thrive in a virtual world devoid of barriers. Individuality, to be sure, is far from extinction, and in many ways the same technology that homogenizes also provides opportunities for meaningful statements of personality. Some have argued this same case in darker terms, going so far as to contend that technology isolates it users and encapsulates them in virtual realities that are inferior to the real one. This said, communication technology, by its very nature, builds connections and obliterates arbitrary, imaginary borders like the Mason-Dixon Line.

Technology is blending Americans into an increasingly undifferentiated mass. Economic globalization does the same in terms of consumption and the lifestyles that emerge from the marketplace. The global economy, in which goods and services take on a transnational quality, rewards interconnectedness and punishes insularity. Products literally come from everywhere and go anywhere. In this process, consumers' wants and needs become generic impulses; one desires what everyone else desires. Northerners and Southerners seek the same satisfaction in a unified market; regional differences become inconsequential. The market not only establishes bonds that transcend map lines; it also encourages both social and physical mobility. A dynamic global market puts people on the move. If the overall scheme remains the same, where one lives or works does not really enter into the equation. Systems dependent on their members staying put, therefore, are first weakened, then extinguished. Globalization, like the Internet, mixes such a vast array of human activities and experiences that the type of reality defined by lines such as the Mason-Dixon seems nothing less than silly.

Whole nations, let alone sections within nations, are being incorporated into a larger, ever more inclusive global community. This translates into an America where the terms *North* and *South* are nearly devoid of meaning and substance. As with some archaic definition passed over in a dictionary, few Americans pay serious attention to regional identifications. The mental concepts that the labels North and South embodied no longer exist, washed away by television, the Internet, and globalization. Northerners gain perspective on world affairs by watching the Southern-based news network CNN. Southerners pattern their social relationships and lifestyles according to a televised reality that reflects the hopes and dreams of Northerners in New York and California. More than one-half of Southern homes have computers in them, and more than one-third of Southerners access the Internet from home. Maryland, one of the founding Southern states, has better access to cyberspace than either New York or its longtime neighbor and rival, Pennsylvania.[80] The South is no longer isolated from the North, and vice versa.

The Northern and Southern economies today are fully integrated. Companies move effortlessly, and without much regard to regional cultures, between the sections, often taking their employees with them. Corporate mobility, as well as the personal mobility it demands, further dilutes regional allegiances and affiliations that linger on as remnants of the America that

Mason and Dixon mapped so carefully. Mobility has also increased the pace of urbanization in the South. Southern cities now rival those in the North in size, diversity, and sophistication. Economically, culturally, and socially, the modern South is in many ways indistinguishable from the North. The line that once cleaved the nation in half persists as a minor tourist attraction incapable of generating much emotion beyond curiosity and nostalgia.

Arbitrary borders can still be drawn. One still hears on occasion declarations such as, "I'm from the ... (North, South, East, West, and so forth)," but such identifications are an echo of the past with no real future. They hearken back to a day when America drew lines to separate mutually incomprehensible worlds. If one is so inclined, one can pencil in lines here and there and claim that they separate something of substance. In truth, borders and boundaries everywhere, especially ones like the Mason-Dixon Line, are losing their descriptive and prescriptive power. In practice and principle, lines are disappearing. The Mason-Dixon Line is illustrative of this process; it has fallen prey to time and change. Once steeped in meaning, the Mason-Dixon Line has come full circle. Once again, it is an almost unknown surveyors' line serving as a simple, unassuming border between Pennsylvania and Maryland.

| | | |
|---|---|---|
| **1632** | | Cecilius Calvert, second Lord Baltimore, receives a royal charter for his proposed colony of Maryland. |
| **1681** | | The king of England grants a colonial charter to William Penn. |
| **1728** | | Charles Mason is born in Gloucestershire, England. |
| **1733** | | Jeremiah Dixon is born in County Durham, England. |
| **1763** | | Mason and Dixon arrive in Philadelphia to begin surveying the border between Pennsylvania and Maryland. |
| **1765** | | After completing the arc around New Castle, Delaware, and the Tangent Line, Mason and Dixon head west to complete their border survey. |
| **1768** | January | The surveyors present their report to the representatives of Pennsylvania and Maryland. Their line becomes the official border between the two colonies. |
| **1768** | September | Mason and Dixon return to England. Mason will make one more trip to America in 1786; Dixon will never see the continent again. |
| **1779** | | Jeremiah Dixon dies successful, but alone, in County Durham. He dedicated himself to his career and never married. |
| **1787** | | The Confederation Congress passes the Northwest Ordinance prohibiting slavery in the lands above the Ohio River won from Great Britain during the Revolution. |
| **1821** | | Missouri is formally admitted into the Union as a slave state. The negotiations of 1820 provide for the exclusion of slavery above the $36^{\circ}30'$ line, which extends from the Mason-Dixon Line through the Louisiana Territory. |
| **1850** | | Henry Clay submits to the Senate his plan for the admission of California into the Union as a free state. His inclusion of a Fugitive Slave Law allows slaveholders to cross the Missouri Compromise Line at will in search of escaped slaves, thus weakening the entire concept of lines of separation between the sections. (California was formally admitted in September 1850.) |

**1854**     Stephen Douglas's Kansas-Nebraska Act is enacted. The act effectively eliminates the 36°30' line as a guide to which areas would be free and which would have slavery. People in the territories would decide the issue themselves under a policy known as "popular sovereignty."

**1858**     Chief Justice of the Supreme Court Roger B. Taney issues a decision in the Dred Scott case. By claiming that Congress had no right to prohibit slavery anywhere in the United States, the decision nullified the Missouri Compromise and convinced many Americans that only war could settle the slavery issue.

**1859**     Daniel Decatur Emmett writes "Dixie," the song that epitomized the Lost Cause and served as the unofficial anthem of the South.

**1763**
Mason and Dixon
arrive in Philadelphia
to begin their survey

**1850**
California admitted as a
free state with the proviso
that slaveholders can
retrieve their fugitive slaves

**1787**
The Confederation
Congress prohibits slavery
above the Ohio River

**1763**          **1854**

**1821**
Missouri is admitted into
the Union as a slave state
(Missouri Compromise)

**1768**
The Mason-Dixon Line
becomes the official border
between Maryland and
Pennsylvania

**1854**
Kansas-Nebraska Act
eliminates the 36° 30'
line as a guide to free
and slaveholding areas

| | |
|---|---|
| **1860** | After the election of Abraham Lincoln, the nominee of the antislavery Republican Party, South Carolina announces that it is seceding from the Union. Soon, ten other Southern states will follow it, forming themselves into the Confederate States of America. |
| **1861** | The Civil War begins with the bombardment of Fort Sumter off the coast of Charleston, South Carolina. |
| **1862** | Lee invades Maryland and is defeated at the battle of Antietam. |
| **1863** | Lee is successful at a second bid to cross the Mason-Dixon Line into Pennsylvania but is defeated once again, this time at Gettysburg. The Confederacy gives up on invading the North and will fight a defensive war from then on. |
| **1865** | Lee surrenders to General Ulysses S. Grant at Appomattox in Virginia, ending the Civil War. |
| **1866** | Edward A. Pollard publishes *The Lost Cause*, popularizing the myth by the same name. |

**1865**
Civil War
ends

**1858**
Decision in Dred Scott
case nullifies the
Missouri Compromise

**1867—c.1950**
Mason-Dixon Line
serves as a perceived
border for the fictional South

1858                    2003

**1861**
Civil War
begins

**c. 1950—present**
Mason-Dixon Line reverts
to being merely the border
between Pennsylvania
and Maryland

**1863**
Lee is successful
in second bid to cross
the Mason-Dixon Line

**1867–c.1950**     The Mason-Dixon Line is revived and serves as a psychological and emotional border for the fictional South known as Dixie. It also marks the transition point between North and South in terms of racial legislation that discriminated against black Americans.

**c.1950–the present**     The Mason-Dixon Line once again acts merely as a border between Pennsylvania and Maryland, its other functions made obsolete by technological, economic, and social changes associated with modernization.

# Chapter 1

1. Garry Wills, *Lincoln at Gettysburg: The Words That Remade America* (New York: Simon and Schuster, 1992), 25.
2. James M. McPherson, *For Cause and Comrades: Why Men Fought in the Civil War* (New York: Oxford University Press, 1997), 95.
3. Henry Steele Commager, ed., *The Blue and the Grey: The Story of the Civil War as Told by Participants* (New York: Wings Books, 1950), 603.

# Chapter 2

4. Jack P. Greene, ed., *Settlements to Society, 1607–1763: A Documentary History of Colonial America* (New York: W. W. Norton and Company, 1975), 20.
5. W. Keith Kavanagh, ed., *Southern Colonies*, vol. III, pt I, *Foundations of Colonial America: A Documentary History* (New York: Chelsea House, 1983), 1698.
6. Gary Nash, *Red, White, and Black: The Peoples of Early America* (Englewood Cliffs, N.J.: Prentice-Hall, 1982), 61.
7. R. C. Simmons, *The American Colonies: From Settlement to Independence* (New York: W. W. Norton and Company, 1976), 43–44.
8. Greene, *Settlements to Society*, 47-48.
9. John J. McCusker and Russell Menard, *The Economy of British America, 1607–1789* (Chapel Hill: University of North Carolina Press, 1985), 119.
10. Edwin J. Perkins, *The Economy of Colonial America* (New York: Columbia University Press, 1980), 51.
11. Greene, *Settlements to Society*, 166–167.
12. Frederick B. Tolles, *Meeting House and Counting House: The Quaker Merchants of Colonial Philadelphia, 1682–1763* (New York: W. W. Norton and Company, 1948), 63.
13. Nash, *Red, White, and Black*, 97.

# Chapter 3

14. Edwin Danson, *Drawing the Line: How Mason and Dixon Surveyed the Most Famous Border in America* (New York: John Wiley and Sons, 2001), 23.
15. McCusker and Menard, *Economy of British America*, 218.
16. Ibid., 121.
17. Perkins, *Economy of Colonial America*, 30–32.
18. McCusker and Menard, *Economy of British America*, 203.
19. Ibid., 222.
20. Ibid., 134.
21. Greene, *Settlements to Society*, 264.
22. Ibid., 250.
23. Perkins, *Economy of Colonial America*, 94.
24. Richard Hofstadter, *America at 1750: A Social Portrait* (New York: Vintage Books, 1973), 153.
25. McCusker and Menard, *Economy of British America*, 131, 136.
26. Greene, *Settlements to Society*, 264.
27. T.H. Breen, *Tobacco Culture: The Mentality of the Great Tidewater Planters on the Eve of the Revolution* (Princeton, N.J.: Princeton University Press, 1985), 82–83.
28. Perkins, *Economy of Colonial America*, 68; Donald R. Wright, *African Americans in the Colonial Era: From African Origins Through the America Revolution* (Arlington Heights, Ill.: Harlan Davidson, 1990), 36–37.
29. James Curtis Ballagh, *White Servitude in the Colony of Virginia: A Study of the System of Indentured Labor in the American Colonies* (New York: Burt Franklin, 1895; reprint, 1969), 62.
30. Edmund S. Morgan, *American Slavery, American Freedom: The Ordeal of Colonial Virginia* (New York: W. W. Norton and Company, 1975), 328.
31. Simmons, *The American Colonies*, 379.

# Chapter 4

32. Danson, *Drawing the Line*, 53.
33. Jack P. Greene, *Peripheries and Center: Constitutional Development in the Extended Politics of the British Empire and the United States, 1607–1788* (New York: W. W. Norton and Company, 1986), 7.
34. Danson, *Drawing the Line*, 54.
35. McCusker and Menard, *Economy of British America*, 133.
36. Ibid., 205.

# Chapter 5

37. Simmons, *The American Colonies*, 178.
38. Ibid., 175–177.

39. Ibid., 175–178.
40. Nash, *Red, White, and Black*, 258.
41. Ibid., 263.
42. *The Journal of Charles Mason and Jeremiah Dixon* (Philadelphia: American Philosophical Society, 1969), 66.
43. *Journal of Charles Mason*, 111.
44. Danson, *Drawing the Line*, 142.

## Chapter 6

45. William M. Wieck, *The Sources of Antislavery Constitutionalism in America, 1760–1848* (Ithaca, N.Y.: Cornell University Press, 1977), 50.
46. Gary B. Nash and Jean R. Soderlund, *Freedom by Degrees: Emancipation in Pennsylvania and Its Aftermath* (New York: Oxford University Press, 1991), xv.
47. Norman K. Risjord, *Chesapeake Politics, 1781–1800* (New York: Columbia University Press, 1978), 217.
48. Ibid., 495.
49. Joyce Appleby, *Capitalism and a New Social Order: The Republican Vision of the 1790s* (New York: New York University Press, 1984), 102.
50. Richard D. Brown, *Modernization: The Transformation of American Life, 1600–1865* (Prospect Heights, Ill.: Waveland Press, 1976), 123.
51. Merrill D. Peterson, *The Great Triumvirate: Webster, Clay, and Calhoun* (New York: Oxford University Press, 1987), 60.

## Chapter 7

52. Brown, Modernization, 183.
53. Oscar Handlin and Lilian Handlin, *Liberty in Expansion, 1760–1850* (New York: Harper and Row, 1989), 36–37.
54. Richard C. Wade, *The Urban Frontier: The Rise of Western Cities, 1790-1830* (Cambridge: Harvard University Press, 1959), 305
55. Handlin and Handlin, *Liberty in Expansion*, 38.
56. Gavin Wright, "'Economic Democracy' and the Concentration of Agricultural Wealth in the Cotton South, 1850–1860," in *The Structure of the Cotton Economy of the Antebellum South*, ed. William Parker

(Washington, D.C.: The Agricultural History Society, 1970), 82.
57. Thomas P. Slaughter, *Bloody Dawn: The Christiana Riot and Racial Violence in the Antebellum North* (New York: Oxford University Press, 1991), ix.
58. William W. Freehling, *The Road to Disunion: Secessionists at Bay, 1776–1854* (New York: Oxford University Press, 1990), 556.

## Chapter 8

59. Kenneth Stampp, ed., *The Causes of the Civil War* (New York: Simon and Schuster, 1991), 111.
60. Ibid., 140.
61. Richard S. Dunn, "Black Society in the Chesapeake, 1776–1810," in *Slavery and Freedom in the Age of the American Revolution*, ed. Ira Berlin andRonald Hoffman (Charlottesville: University of Virginia Press, 1983), 63.
62. "We'll Be Free in Our Maryland," *America Singing: Nineteenth-Century Song Sheets, The Library of Congress.* Online. 19 June 2003.
63. James M. McPherson, *Battle Cry of Freedom: The Civil War Era* (New York: Oxford University Press, 1988), 284.
64. James M. McPherson, *Ordeal by Fire: The Civil War* (New York: Alfred A. Knopf, 1982), 152.
65. McPherson, *Battle Cry of Freedom*, 535.
66. Ibid., 534.
67. Ibid., 536.
68. Ibid., 544–545.
69. Roy Blount, Jr., "Making Sense of Robert E. Lee," *Smithsonian* (July 2003), 64.

## Chapter 9

70. William Ecenbarger, *Walkin' the Line: A Journey From Past to Present Along the Mason-Dixon* (New York: M. Evans and Company, 2000), 111.
71. Peter S. Carmichael, "New South Visionaries: Virginia's Last Generations of Slaveholders, the Gospel of Progress, and the Lost Cause," in *The Myth of the Lost Cause and Civil War History*, ed. Gary W. Gallagher and Alan T. Nolan

(Bloomington: Indiana University Press, 2000), 116.

72. Ibid. (introduction), 8.73. Steve Levin, "'Dixie' now too symbolic of old South, not of origins," *post-gazette.com* PG News, . 4 September 1998, 3. <http://www.post-gazette.com/regionstate/19980904dixie4.asp>. Online. 19 June 2003.0

74. Ibid., 2.

75. Lloyd A. Hunter, "The Immortal Confederacy: Another Look at Lost Cause Religion," in Gallagher and Nolan, *Myth of the Lost Cause,* 186.

76. Stampp, *Causes of the Civil War,* 202–205.

77. Eric Foner, *Reconstruction: America's Unfinished Revolution, 1863–1877* (New York: Harper and Row, 1988), 422.

## Chapter 10

78. Wills, *Lincoln at Gettysburg,* 40.

79. Henry Steele Commager, ed., *Documents of American History,* vol. 1 (New York: Appleton-Century-Crofts, 1958), 443.

80. United States Census Bureau, *Statistical Abstract of the United States,* Section 24: Communication and Information Technology (No. 1126. Utilization of Selected Media: 1970–1999; No. 1159. Household with Computers and Internet Access:1998–2000); Section 1: Population (No. 25. Annual Inmigration, Outmigration, and Net Migration for Regions: 1990–1999; No. 30. Metropolitan and Nonmetropolitan Area Population by State: 1980–2000); Current Population Survey, August 2000. Online.

Appleby, Joyce. *Capitalism and a New Social Order: The Republican Vision of the 1790s.* New York: New York University Press, 1984.

Ballagh, James Curtis. *White Servitude in the Colony of Virginia: A Study of the System of Indentured Labor in the American Colonies.* New York: Burt Franklin, 1895; reprint, 1969.

Blount, Roy Jr. "Making Sense of Robert E. Lee." *Smithsonian* (July 2003): 58–65.

Breen, T.H. *Tobacco Culture: The Mentality of the Great Tidewater Planters on the Eve of the Revolution.* Princeton, N.J.: Princeton University Press, 1985.

Brown, Richard D. *Modernization: The Transformation of American Life, 1600–1865.* Prospect Heights, Ill.: Waveland Press, 1976.

Carmichael, Peter S. "New South Visionaries: Virginia's Last Generation of Slaveholders, the Gospel of Progress, and the Lost Cause." In *The Myth of the Lost Cause and Civil War History,* edited by Gary W. Gallagher and Alan T. Nolan, 111–126. Bloomington: Indiana University Press, 2000.

Commager, Henry Steele, ed. *The Blue and the Grey: The Story of the Civil War as Told by Participants.* New York: Wings Books, 1950.

———. *Documents of American History.* New York: Appleton-Century-Crofts, Inc., 1958.

Danson, Edwin. *Drawing the Line: How Mason and Dixon Surveyed the Most Famous Border in America.* New York: John Wiley and Sons, 2001.

Dunn, Richard S. "Black Society in the Chesapeake, 1776–1810." In *Slavery and Freedom in the Age of the American Revolution,* edited by. Ira Berlin and Ronald Hoffman, 49–82. Charlottesville: University of Virginia Press, 1983.

Ecenbarger, William. *Walkin' the Line: A Journey From Past to Present Along the Mason-Dixon.* New York: M. Evans and Company, 2000.

Foner, Eric. *Reconstruction: America's Unfinished Revolution, 1863–1877.* New York: Harper and Row, 1988.

Freehling, William W. *The Road to Disunion: Secessionists at Bay, 1776–1854.* New York: Oxford University Press.

Gallagher, Gary W. Introduction. to *The Myth of the Lost Cause and Civil War History,* edited by Gary W. Gallagher and Alan T. Nolan, 1–9. Bloomington: Indiana University Press, 2000.

Greene, Jack P., ed. *Settlements to Society, 1607–1763: A Documentary History of Colonial America.* New York: W.W. Norton and Company, 1975.

———. *Peripheries and Center: Constitutional Development in the Extended Politics of the British Empire and the United States, 1607–1788.* New York: W. W. Norton and Company, 1986.

Handlin, Oscar, and Lilian Handlin. *Liberty in Expansion, 1760–1850.* New York: Harper and Row, 1989.

Hunter, Lloyd A. "The Immortal Confederacy: Another Look at the Lost Cause Religion." In *The Myth of the Lost Cause and Civil War History,* edited by Gary W. Gallagher and Alan T. Nolan, 185–218. Bloomington: Indiana University Press, 2000.

Kavanaugh, W. Keith, ed. *Foundations of Colonial America: A Documentary History.* 3 vols. New York: Chelsea House, 1983.

Levin, Steve. "'Dixie' now too symbolic of the old South, not of origins." *Post-gazette.com PG News,* 4 September 1998. <http://www.post-gazette.com/regionstate/19980904dixie4.asp>. Online. 19 June 2003.

Levine, Bruce. *Half Slave, Half Free: The Roots of the Civil War.* New York: Hill and Wang, 1992.

Martin, John Frederick. *Profits in the Wilderness: Entrepreneurship and the Founding of the New England Towns in the Seventeenth Century.* Chapel Hill: University of North Carolina Press, 1991.

Mason, A. Hewlett, ed. *The Journal of Charles Mason and Jeremiah Dixon.* Philadelphia: American Philosophical Society, 1969.

McCusker, John J., and Russell Menard. *The Economy of British America, 1607–1789.* Chapel Hill: University of North Carolina Press, 1985.

McPherson, James M. *Ordeal by Fire*. 3 vols. New York: Alfred A. Knopf, 1982.

————. *Battle Cry of Freedom: The Civil War Era*. New York: Oxford University Press, 1988.

————. *For Cause and Comrades: Why Men Fought in the Civil War*. New York: Oxford University Press, 1997.

Middlekauff, Robert. *The Glorious Cause: The American Revolution, 1763–1789*. New York: Oxford University Press, 1982.

Morgan, Edmund S. *American Slavery, America Freedom: The Ordeal of Colonial Virginia*. New York: W.W. Norton and Company, 1975.

Nash, Gary. *Red, White, and Black: The Peoples of Early America*. Englewood Cliffs, N.J.: Prentice-Hall, 1982.

———— and Jean R. Soderlund. *Freedom by Degrees: Emancipation in Pennsylvania and Its Aftermath*. New York: Oxford University Press, 1991.

Perkins, Edwin J. *The Economy of Colonial America*. New York: Columbia University Press, 1980.

Peterson, Merrill D. *The Great Triumvirate: Webster, Clay, and Calhoun*. New York: Oxford University Press, 1987.

Risjord, Norman K. *Chesapeake Politics, 1781–1800*. New York: Columbia University Press, 1978.

Simmons, R.C. *The American Colonies: From Settlement to Independence*. New York: W.W. Norton and Company, 1976.

Slaughter, Thomas P. *Bloody Dawn: The Christiana Riot and Racial Violence in the Antebellum North*. New York: Oxford University Press, 1991.

Stampp, Kenneth, ed. *The Causes of the Civil War*. New York: Simon and Schuster, 1991.

Tolles, Frederick B. *Meeting House and Counting House: The Quaker Merchants of Colonial Philadelphia, 1682–1763*. New York: W.W. Norton and Company, 1948.

United States Census Bureau. *Statistical Abstract of the United States,* Section 24: Information and Communication, 2001 (No. 1126. Utilization of Selected Media: 1970–1999; No. 1159. Households with Computers and Internet Access). Online.

————. *Statistical Abstract of the United States,* Section 1: Population, 2001 (No. 26. Mobility Status of the Population by Selected Characteristics; No.30. Metropolitan and Nonmetropolitan Area Population by State: 1980–2000). Online.

Wieck, William M. *The Sources of Antislavery Constitutionalism in America, 1760–1848.* Ithaca, N.Y.: Cornell University Press, 1977.

Wills, Garry. *Lincoln at Gettysburg: The Words That Remade America.* New York: Simon and Schuster, 1992.

Wright, Donald R. *African Americans in the Colonial Era: From African Origins Through the American Revolution.* Arlington Heights, Ill.: Harlan Davidson, 1990.

Wright, Gavin. "'Economic Democracy' and the Concentration of Agricultural Wealth in the Cotton South, 1850–1860." In *The Structure of the Cotton Economy in the Antebellum South,* edited by William Parker, 63–93. Washington, D.C.: The Agricultural History Society, 1970.

*America, 1859–1863.* New York: W. W. Norton and Company, 2003.

Bell, Whitfield J., Jr. *Patriot-Improvers: Biographical Sketches of the Members of the American Philosophical Society.* Vol. 1, 1743–1768, *Memoirs of the American Philosophical Society.* Philadelphia: American Philosophical Society, 1997.

Danson Edwin. "Mason, Charles and Jeremiah Dixon." *American National Biography Online*, January 2000. <http://www.anb.org/articles/13/13-o2640-article.html>. Online. 14 May 2003.

O'Hara, Daniel. "Biography of Jeremiah Dixon." *ThomasPynchon.com.* <http://hyperarts.com/pynchon/mason-dixon/extra/dixon_bio.html>. Online. 14 May 2003.

Pynchon, Thomas. *Mason and Dixon.* New York: Henry Holt, 1997.

Romeo, Richard. "Biography of Charles Mason." *ThomasPynchon.com.* <http://hyperarts.com/pynchon/mason-dixon/extra/mason_bio.html>.Online. 14 May 2003.

Sobel, Dava. *Longitude: The True Story of a Lone Genius Who Solved the Greatest Scientific Problem of His Time.* N.P.: Fourth Estate, 1996.

St. George, Judith. *Mason and Dixon's Line of Fire.* New York: Putnam, 1991.

page:

FM Courtesy of the Library of Congress
Geography & Map Division

3 Courtesy of the Library of Congress,
LC-USZ62-3282

10 Courtesy of the Library of Congress
Geography & Map Division

18 Courtesy of the Library of Congress

23 Courtesy of the Library of Congress,
LC-USZ62-3282

31 ©Bettman/CORBIS

39 ©Image Select/Art Resource, NY

50 ©CORBIS

55 Courtesy of the Library of Congress,
LC-B8171-3608

61 Courtesy of the Library of Congress
Geography & Map Division

64 Courtesy of the Library of Congress,
LC-USZ62-23836

68 Courtesy of the John Rankin House
Collection, Ohio Historical Center
Archives Library

76 Courtesy of the Library of Congress

80 Courtesy of the Library of Congress,
LC-BH82-2417

84 Courtesy of the Library of Congress,
LC-B8184-841

91 Courtesy of the Library of Congress,
LC-USZ62-115416 DLC

101-Courtesy of the Library of Congress,
HABS, PA, 1-ZORA.V,1-1

Cover Courtesy of the Library of Congress
Geography & Map Division

**John C. Davenport** holds a Ph.D. from the University of Connecticut and currently teaches at Corte Madera School in Portola Valley, California. He lives in San Carlos, California, with his wife, Jennifer, and his two sons, William and Andrew.

**George J. Mitchell** served as chairman of the peace negotiations in Northern Ireland during the 1990s. Under his leadership, an historic accord, ending decades of conflict, was agreed to by the governments of Ireland and the United Kingdom and the political parties in Northern Ireland. In May 1998, the agreement was overwhelmingly endorsed by a referendum of the voters of Ireland, North and South. Senator Mitchell's leadership earned him worldwide praise and a Nobel Peace Prize nomination. He accepted his appointment to the U.S. Senate in 1980. After leaving the Senate, Senator Mitchell joined the Washington, D.C. law firm of Piper Rudnick, where he now practices law. Senator Mitchell's life and career have embodied a deep commitment to public service and he continues to be active in worldwide peace and disarmament efforts.

**James I. Matray** is professor of history and chair at California State University, Chico. He has published more than forty articles and book chapters on U.S.-Korean relations during and after World War II. Author of *The Reluctant Crusade: American Foreign Policy in Korea, 1941–1950 and Japan's Emergence as a Global Power,* his most recent publication is *East Asia and the United States: An Encyclopledia of Relations Since 1784.* Matray also is international columnist for the *Donga Ilbo* in South Korea.